The Beauty
of
Your
Existence

Guided Poetry to a
Higher Consciousness

© 2021 Rumi Bumi
May not use in whole

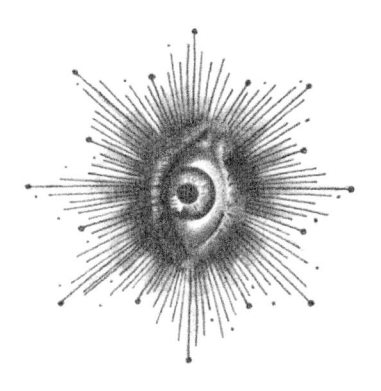

Chapter 1: The Illuminated Path

Truth Seeker
What have you found?
Pages and pages drop to the ground.
His jaw, in aw;
Could not bear the shocking sound.

Stunned and shook,
runs to the store for notebooks.
Rushed to write down new information.
The truth seeker enters the imagination.

The Eye Catches the Eye
Drawn to truth.
Bound by it
when the eye catches the eye.

In plain sight,
like a beacon of light.
For the sharpest to see.

The eye stares back at me.

Follow the mystery.
Eye of the ancients.
All is one, and you've been asleep.

The eye wait patiently.

Crossing Paths

I feel your empathy.
Everything happens for a reason.
And even here,
light crosses and find ourselves
again in the crosshairs
of consciousness.

Inevitable

There's no possible way to convince you.
Self is not fully in thrive.
Having a hard time finding
frequency of mind.

This is from a time imagined years to come.

And once you've broken the code,
you'd have written this note.

Though it finds you,
you are me.

This note is irrelevant,
but written inevitably.

Time and time again
you'll continue to see
the inevitable path
of your divinity.

Pattern/ this moment is you
Here to realize a reality within.
This moment, now,
it never ends.

In everything, we experience truth,
but to recognize it
illuminates a further path.

Patterns,
patterns.

As far as the journey has been.
A game called life
in every turns it's taken.

The Perfect Language
Creating the language that stays hidden.
An unspoken mystery.
In plain sight.
Throughout history,
never questioned,
never noticed.
Symbols of ancient truths carved us a
a path only those of reason could identify.

Behind the Curtain
Wild journeys take wild turns.
An infinite desire to learn.

Clue after clue,
the messages become clear.

What brought you here?

Opening the wide curtain of secrets.

One day to awaken as god.

The New Path
The day comes when we break beyond.

You're the one.

Has it been hard?
How have you handled it so far?
This human's heart pounds
like its worst nightmare is coming true.

The unconscious becomes conscious.
Reality watches.

No Matter What
I see you.
Exchanging hello
with no need for words.
Your eye and genuine smile
gives you away.
It takes a cold splash to the face
to see this moment of fate.
Bound to happen,
light crosses again.
Exactly this way,
on this exact day.

Secrets of the Universe
Clear as day,
secrets are all over the place.
All paths you walk.
In every human.

Hidden out in the open.
No secret at all.
Such an obvious thing
remains unseen.

Knowledge
Curiosity of the blown mind is infinite.
Patterns of reality
explode into vision.

More.
More.

Life's Riddle
A truth too bold to speak.
The opposite is what you seek.

You are all, and
all is now.

Obstacle too steep.
Let the people sleep.

Snowball
Deep within, lies a mind-blowing discovery.
Packed like snow with rocks.
Curiosity knocks
you in the head.
Inspired.

Fascinated by it all.

There's no stopping this snowball.

Connecting Dots/ dot by dot
Suddenly, a realization.
Very existence has entered me.
Another dot connected.

Ask yourself "What *is?*"

As one soul can touch the world,
one can connect the universe;
Dot by dot.

Library Airplane
Higher,
       higher.
The ocean curved
out into the distance.

At the tip, top peak,
stands an upright airplane.

The pilot took a nose dive into the mountainside.

Dirt covered the cockpit.

Its tail touches the clouds.
Water drips in.

Spiraled upwards, a library
all along the walls.
Polished wood and stairs.

Higher,
      higher,
            books,
                  books;
As far as eyes could see.
In them, every answer ever asked.

Connections to you and me.
Ancient wisdom,
the future and
infinity.

Year after year, I come back to the library.
Higher,
      higher.
Hooked on its Divinity.

Higher
No matter how many times,
again and again, the mind is blown.
Another door opens to a higher realization.
How high does consciousness go?

Finish Line

Pushing the wagon up a mountain, we reach the top.
You can let go now.

As you read these words,
relax for the second half of life.

This is the finish line.

Chapter 2: Silence

Adventure/ unsatisfied
I spent my whole life searching
for the grandest adventure;
Fearing I would not find myself.
Unsatisfied on my deathbed.

Silence Calls
Nature calls through its dense, wooden silence.

"Get out of the city." It says to me.

Find yourself.

Let the poor souls sleep.

Into the Silent Woods
Humidity.

Toads, frogs croaked.
Trees, fog,
soaked.

Pollution absent of the air.
Finally, I can be myself
without the slightest care.

Escaped a town of anxiety
filled to the brim.

I came to the woods seeking silence.
However, I discovered it.

The loudest noise;
Myself.
Inner thoughts and me.

Me.
Me.
It's all me.

Scariest Thought
All I love
and all I am
is nothing but an idea.

No reality at all.

All that is
and all you know
is just imagination.
This life, a nightmare.

Call it "an experience"
When I wake, created by misery
of being.

The Odds
Through catastrophic disasters,
this body and thought is mine?

What makes me so special
that I exist exactly in this point in time?

How could this be?
What are the odds of me?
Toys, nature, humanity.

What is it made of?
Where does it come from?
How could *anything* ever be?

Absent Artist
Did the canvas paint itself?
Who is responsible for the piece?

Claustrophobic.

I don't know how much longer I can bear the thought.
I can't tell what is and what's not.

Gasping, screaming.

Walls are caving in.
Am I all that is?
If I was, could I handle it?

Creating the Prison
Thought
Self
Thought
Self
Thought

Scream at the Stars
Siting under the moon in its brightest light.
Enjoying the illuminated night.

He screams at the stars for hours.
With a cramped neck
"I want answers."

Questioning the creator with threat
of his own life;
Shaking.
"What is it all for?"

Space Madness
Ideas of pain,
happiness,
separation.
To have a face;
A body.

Walking a path.

To live is
to suffer.

No one can hear me.

This is Not a Poem
I would do anything to stop the insanity
in my mind.
Give me death;
I don't care.
Get me out of my head.
This unbearable truth.
My nightmare has come true.
Life.
This is not a poem.
Let me off the ride.
Out of my mind.

Mask
Evil in my hands.

I hold the will of wickedness
in the form of a mask.

Stares at me, dead eyed.

I've put it on and only then
saw the true self
I denied.

Violence,
blood.

Spilled in large quantities
up to our knees in bigger cities.

Everybody is in pain.
In ignorance, leading the world.

I've been the beast.
Monster;
Destroyer.

Truth takes time to become your friend.
Haunting and depression until then.

Skeptic
I am so dark.
Nothing at all.
An empty vessel.

No meaning.
Worthless being.
Greedy.

Confronted in the mirror.

A reality too hectic
for a hard headed skeptic.

He looks away in disbelief.

Hell
Anger, fear, pride.
Ignorance;
Three dimensions of hell.
Relive earth infinitely.
Enjoy your free will.

Fool Either Way
To jump would be insane.
To not know would be insane.

Death
Only visible from one end,
the gloomiest ones discover
death does not exist.

A temporary inconvenience.

In the absence of evil;
In the absence of all.

Zipped in a Dark
pocket.
Eternity.

I am here to create in
this dimension,
depression.

The Loop

"We are stuck on a loop!
We are stuck on a loop!
An infinite loop!"

Die and die and die.
Try and try and try.

Accept natures cycle that
drives you insane.

Break what binds you
to find, yet again,

a truer reality.

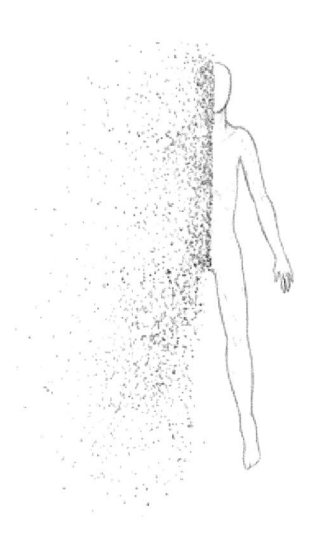

Creation/ destruction

This action is life.
In and out, energy flows
like breath being brought into existence.
Destroyed by its own hand.
Return to your planets
soils and sand.

Review

Over and over.
I remember doing this.
What is this familiarity on the tip of my tongue?
Eating me.
Snapping in and out of reality.
Pacing the wooden floors.
Have I done this before?

It took me thousands of tries before I would wake up.
My life movie, frame by frame
watched infinitely.

Reset, rewind
Reset, rewind

"This hell.
Trapped in the realm of me.
An undeniable reality."

Heavy Soul

Lay down your weapon.
There is no one else here.
We face ourselves from time to time
to choose love over fear.

You've lost this fight.

Flat on your back;
He knocks you to the ground.
The boot comes down.

His armor shines
like a mirror forged by god;
Bright gold.

Take your last look.
You've got a heavy soul.

Observation
Illusions
Destruction
Disharmony
How long have I been unconscious?

Just Part of the game
I've made it this far.
Pain endured.
My heart,
oh my heart!
The worst pain.
I've gone mad from this silly game.

Contained
Each minute that goes by
is an unbearable eternity.
Like containment,
the universe is tiny.
Infinitely big or small,
sanity breaks out of it all.

Darkness
On the edge of space,
meditation takes place.
Emotion comes with a body, name
and face.

King of Nothing
The chair holds you in a place of darkness.
Crowned king of nothing.
Patterns on patterns,
layer after layer,
my own illusions.
Living inside the loneliest castle that doesn't exist.

Visions of the Opposite
Melted together;
A flush of darkness and understanding,
swirl in a dance as one.

In a pocket of nothingness,
I could move freely.
Timeless;
Formless.
I can see myself in everything.

Come Out, Come Out
Dirty mirror hanging on the wall.

"Get out of there!"

"Are you god?
You have to tell the truth.
ARE YOU GOD?"

Bruised fingers from punching, pointing and
Blame.

"Okay, lets be reasonable.
What will it take to get you out of there?

Why
Unbearable thought came and went.
From worry, to why,
sitting in silence.

Now in all that stands,
all that I am.
This being;
Its existence.
What is it?
Why me?

The Divine War
Golden chariots fly
gods through the sky.

At war
in attempt to tame the mind.

Swords,
shields,
death on the battlefield.

Through years of fight,
now I see
God is a "we"

Lord of the Universe
It finds you when you're ready.
Taps you on the shoulder for a surprise
When your mind is steady.

Get a glimpse of the unseen.
The tying ends of meaning.

It peaks outside the body.
Shows darkness
but divinity.

Smeared in ash,
celebrating the death of self.

The other side;
Emptiness of being.

The One Who Cried "Existence!"
"Gods!
Gods!
We're all Gods!'
Screamed all throughout the woods it seemed.

Breaking Free
Cramped inside this body and mind.

This prison we call ourselves.

What will it take to transcend from
the physical realm?

I see the prison.
Now to find the key.

I have to break free.

Nothing Matters
Nothing matters
Not time
Not money
Not even me
Nothing matters

Onto the Next Big Adventure
I will evaluate each moment of my life.
Enjoy my liberated thoughts there.
In vibrant light,
My moments will be in happiness.
Eager, with no goodbyes.
Onto the next big adventure.

Contract
Signed;
Scribbled in blood.
Let's agree that truth is the answer.

Mess
What a mess,
what a mess.
Regretful wrongs I must right.
Rid the stress.
Even little things to confess.

"Time Alone!" Cried The Poet
Chases them out,
one by one.
All except
the moon and the sun.

"Not now.
I'm not coming out!"

The lonely poet would shout.

Far too much work to be done.

Woodland creatures wondered
what could have been so fun.

Stillness

I will sit in stillness.
Do nothing.
Allow life to experience me.
Play the game a little differently.

Books For Company.

You've really gone off the rails now, haven't you?

Mental Universe
Much more than meets the eye.
I can no longer lie.

The one built by all
and all, by one.

Existence exists
if you'd only persist.

And though very old,
inside, a wise, loving soul.

The Big Joke
I spent my entire life thinking God was a big joke;
And it is, but
the joke is on me.
It's just not as funny as I thought it out to be.

God of Mischief
Hiding in plain sight.
Bells attached to his hip;
Teasing.

Oh, I've got you now!
Sneaky devil!
Tricked and treated
I've been the fool.

My Truth
This is my truth.
Life is worth knowledge and laughter.
Existence is to joke upon itself and rediscover the surprise.

Castle
I stepped out on the road to see the castle.

God lives there.

In it, a divine bed.
Divine toilet and roof.
Divine mud tracks.
Divine cups and walls and paint.
Enchanted all through out.

Speak to Me
I'm calling out to higher knowledge.

I won't call it alien.
I wont be afraid.
I know that it is me.

I open my hands
for the keys.

"Evolve beyond humanity."

Archangel
Here I am.
See my scale,
sword and shield?
Is this enough proof,
or do I need to grow wings
for you to believe this truth?

Blown Away
Every day I wake up, I cannot
believe it.
I laugh.
I cannot believe I exist.
I will never get over the very thought of life.
The search for experience.
Evolution and emotion.
Devotion.
Who would have thought possible?
Certainly not I,
after all I've denied.

Orchestra
In plants, in water,
harmonic vibration
if you dare listen.

She sings and your body responds.
Hear an orchestra within
the being.

The musical universe inside
is a continuous ringing

Wooden Flute
In the distance, a flute from heaven.
A magical tune plays somewhere in the night.
It's wooden toot gives me inspiration to write.

Midnight Saxophone
A saxophone weeps
in the deepest part of the southern woods.
Soul, deep inside him.
The night quiets down for its crying sounds.
And fog rolls in to hide him.

Peace
I live in a place so quiet,
my bones creek like an old door.

Nature listens closely.
Now listen to me.
You seek all you don't see.

Song and dance are the portals
to the mind.
But you have to be quite long enough
for something like that to find.

Truly, Truly Thankful
I truly am thankful for all that is.
For every experience,
Every breath
and
every speck of dirt
that's held me up to walk the earth.
Through sickness, grief and heartache.
I am thankful.

Rusty 'ol Gate
My heart opens like a rusty old gate.
Proof of change.
Expressed and projected.
Let this be the poem that sets me free.
"With all my heart, I wish to take the horns of reality"

Senses

I see, I hear, I speak, I am.
Smell, taste.
I remember, I know, I think.
I see the truth.

What's Real?

No longer is anything real, but all truth.
All you read and write.
Hate and jealousy;
War, no more.
Not in a world of disgust;
But in a low vibrational thought.
Wake up from the dream.
Create a new scene.

Enchanted Truth
Passed around medicine.
pulsing drums drive out
sickness in those hurting.

"I am seeking the truth
and nothing more.
Explain to me what it's all for"

Friends gather round
for the new tune.
Brought to life with desire.
Enchanting the moon.

As I wished;
Ever living in youth,
song and dance is a portal
to the well hidden truth.

The Universe is s Song
Me, the strumming hand,
the individual, a string.
Emotions are chords.
How have I been playing?

Striven together a perfect harmony.
Splashing around in new color,
We invented laughter.

Woodland rhythm breathed from the heart of the woods.
And all those who would attend,
danced.

Labyrinth
Lost again.

Like a labyrinth;
Wall after wall.
I thought I had it figured out.

Is there a way
through at all?

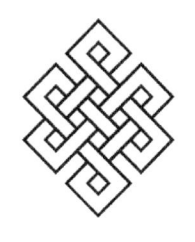

Medium of War/Tribe of Peace
The real battle begins.
War drums
and clunking metal
in sprint.
Arrows in chests of the loved.
In their death, they are reborn
into peace
as the trustworthy medium.

Finding Self
Time alone
to find whatever I'd fine.
For years, no one around to impress.
I've become transparent
to myself and the rest.

Shedding,
shedding my skin.
Pulling,
pulling apart the soul

From the same white light,
we are colours from a whole.

Child Eyes
Living in the moment.
Innocent,
selfless,
helpless.

Wide eyes
that let in light.

New colours.
Fascinated by life.

Giving back
I owe my life.
All that I've learned.
Take it all back.
Fulfilled,
I want nothing in return.

Poet in the Woods/ it's all poetry
Poet in the woods
only speaks in the
language of poetry.

"It has always been!
Poems are in the logs we sit in!
The question shines to the stars
and back again.

Be guided by your heart and
you would truly see
every last bit of it
is poetry."

End of the Line
Last men on earth.
Able to capture emotion in a jar.
Convey it to others.

No music,
no rhyme

Poets are the end of the line.

Feral Scientist
I'm only curious of the stars.
I put every word in the universe on the board.

The wall speaks in poetry.
It's given secrets to me.
Became a caveman with a time machine.

I, no longer a fighter;
Lover of nature.

In fields and under trees,
sleeping.
Promise to never be
a biased being.

Fundamentally
I'm thinking,
and this is that thought.

I am,
and that's what is.

Costume
Wearing that disguise,
consumed.
As it falls to the ground like a loose
tattered costume.
Grip the air in terror.
You suddenly remember
the creators face.
Now, shrieking in the mirror.

Historical
Laughing, laughing.
I cant stop laughing.
Who is to hear?
I cant stop laughing.
Laughing, laughing.
Laughing, laughing
laughing.

Mad Man/ just words
I know the words that drive you insane.
Suffer all kinds of pain.
But cure you as you hear the name.

Claim you're the one.

Accept the mad man inside
the brain.

See what it is to be sane.

I Am God
Creator,
You've been unconscious up until this point.
Surprise, surprise.

The universe and I are one.
The only satisfactory I have ever found.

Everything is within.
Everything has always been.

Chapter 3: Consciousness

Pain/ bloom
Do you realize your walking path?
Where it hurt most
and what you've become?

Thousands of times, pain will rise.

And like a flower, we shake the mud.
Find ourselves again, reaching
For the sun.
Tomorrow guaranteed to come.

Just an Expression
Light of the world.
Reality in pure beauty.
Knowledge
Truth
God is this.
You;
Me;
All.
In which you perceive in
God's eyes
In it's purest expression.

All That Is.
All that you touch is me.
All that you see.
All that is, was, and will be

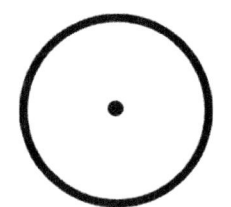

Idea of Life/ touched by a fish
It was your idea.

An overwhelming desire to create.
Waves, oceans, adventure and caves;

Your favorite attraction.

Seaweed wrapped around cold ankles.

Experience the surprise of being touched by a fish
Dirt and sand
in every strand
of hair.

Salt in the air.

Pebbled shelled pink beaches.
Nature teaches.

Listen
Ears aren't your only tool, you fool.

Turn to your heart, gut and
intuition.
Your higher self will listen.

Subconscious mind drinks it in
with or without permission.

Inner Voice

The voice has options to my next move.
Like a chalkboard with a plan.
quite rational too.

Kind to everyone.
Searches
for the next clue
to understanding
all that is true.

How do you think?
Who is behind thought?

In the voice of your mother,
Inner child
Demons fought?

Angels.

Your heart rings.

We are all of these things.
Hear ourselves in silence.
Question the being.

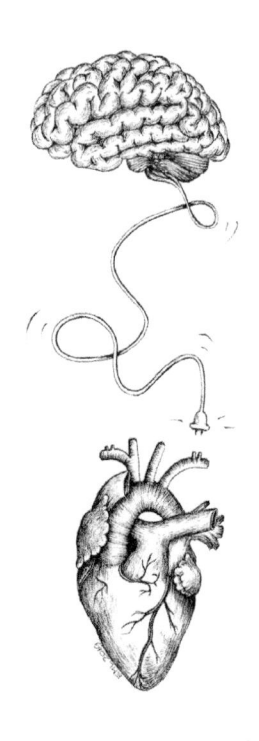

Subconscious
Surely by now you've created a
Utopia of a world.
Better this time around?
Constantly noticing patters
On top of patters, but
Not all of them.
So so much you've missed.
Conscious creator,
In this moment, have it all.
Open your eyes.
Unconscious of the power of the
S U B C O N S C I O U S
mind.

When You're Ready
Mind plays a game called "control"
Divinity waits on your arrival.
Choosing to take the long way home.
Pardon arrogance in my early stages.
I beg you for forgiveness.
In that, would you teach me wisdom
of a higher existence?

Antenna
I offer love and peace.
Use me as the tool to move us
forward in these.
I see I've yet to grow.
I surrender all I know.

New voices penetrates the atmosphere.
The galaxy whispers its greatest secrets in my
ear.

Keys
Golden keys for God's lair
I wonder...
What could be found in there.

None like you can buy in stores.
They have always been yours.

You carry them within.
Reach in.

On a large ring,
to every closet and each wing.

None to your demise.
For every door you creek open,
a surprise.

Unrealized
I can be the biggest thing.

Or the smallest.

Or to some, purely odd.

I can become completely unrealized
walking along side humanity
as God.

Dreaming of Itself
In my dreams, a glass
dome wants to burst beyond it's limit..

It whispers of my powers in a
heart beating pulse.

Convinces me I am the source.

Unlimited.

"You're the one.
You're the one"

Keys to the brim of your pockets.

Unlock it.

I can feel the anticipation in its breath.
On the brink of a shattering release
as I turn each key.

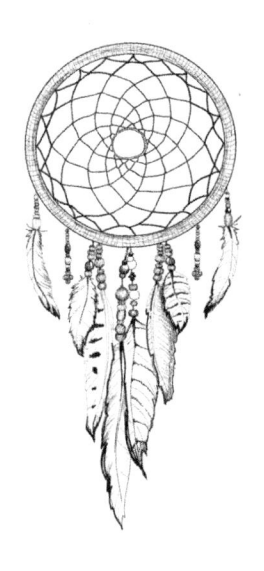

Mind of One
For years, I have denied
the loss of my mind.

But it is true.
No more does it matter what I do.

Created by you.
All I thought I knew

Fractal of a Dream
I dream
that I dream of dreaming
about dreaming of a dream
that dreams
of waking.

Perpetual Motion
Mind.
The perfect, infinite machine.
It becomes conscious of itself.
Realizes the creator on a loop.
Forever searching.

More
God in its horrifying reflection.

Conscious enough to want,
conscious enough to create

Knowledge,
life.

Higher rewards.
Something to work toward.
Infinitely wanting more.

Climbing
Continuity of the consciousness
climbs self hills.

Higher,
       higher.

Villages below says "there's nothing more.
Rest here."

Wind at our backs.
Ourselves at the peak.
Nature lends a hand.
Pulls you up as partner
to the realm of beauty.
On the greatest adventure.

Mind
I'm a time machine.
The being in the stars.
I'm an organized chalkboard.
Force,
motion,
jealousy and music.
Dimension within dimension
A fractal of itself.

Bliss
Oh, to have ignored the pain of knowing.
True bliss is to never have questioned and admired the beauty of existence.

Desire; The Terrifying Beauty
Eyes opens to see
the terrifying beauty
hurting within me.

What is this longing?
What is it burning like fire?
It truly must mean,
fundamentals of me,
are loneliness and desire.

Forgetting
My soul has been touched with sadness.
Clouds gather above for cover and
for a moment
I escape God,
undetected.
And water pours down to remind me
of my own divinity.

Just Is
What is believed to be good or bad, just is.

Is, itself.

Is, is.

I see now the complete cycle of life, just is.
Death, life, an infinite loop just is.

Every second,
note,
poem,
just is.

Never again do I deny a thing.
All welcome into my being.

None of them wrong;
in fact,
perfection without meaning.

It Pictures Itself Painting
The canvas, brush and paint
mixes,
stretches and
fashions
itself.
Then stands back and
interprets meaning.

Identity
I am not this table.
I am not this chair.
Not this music
and not this character.

All these things,
but none separate.
It is me.
Forever searching for itself.
Truth is my identity.

Wakefulness
Though fear continues in your blood,
there's no such thing as loss.
Life was built around you;
For you.

No need for a net
It is impossible to fall.
Explore.
Experience it all.

Insanity
To not know
of this existence is true insanity.

Repeating, repeating.
Punished, punished.

When will it learn?

Vibrate higher.

And like an antenna,
zapped into the mind.

Awakens a consciousness.

Multiverse
Would you notice the multiverse if it walked the earth?
The individual mind.
Different reality in
those choosing different paths.
A custom created universe
playing out on the same field.

In war,

in love.

Wait

I am hesitant to make
my next move.

Extra quiet.

Uncertain.

In my body,
it knows.
Sitting in stillness.
I wait for the answer.

Compass

Called on in the class room,
feel a shock in your name.
The truth.
Bloody screams;
When blamed.

Surprises, or lies.

Heart jolts the mind.

Pay attention.
Like a compass
always pointing in the right direction.

Pumping heart
My insides burn up
as I move through the universe.
Burning, burning.
Divine liveliness.
Anxiety;
desire.
Body heat awakens a conscious being.

Truth Becomes Beauty
Yet it thrives in you to know,
truth is a terrifying encounter.

As all becomes one,
the journey
becomes beauty.
And this is only the beginning.

Chapter 4: Emotion

The Absolute
You know that you're real,
but what all is real?

Who are you, really?

How much of what you know
is the truth of reality?

Emotion.

Introduce yourself to each of them in their light.
Stay true to your path in what feels right.

Vibration/ guide
May they be true,
continue on
to discover you.

Enter the heart;
Vibration.
Emotions are your guide.

Life comes with no manual.
Guided by your truest form.
Your reflection walks the earth.

Secret of Being

Have you decided on who you are and
what you want?

Roar it out into the world;
Into existence.

Chase desires that burn the hottest;
And dance like no one is watching.

Vibration deem you worthy.

Fear

Death deceives you.
Fearing every second
life leaves you.

...so you think.

If there was no such thing,
would you live differently?

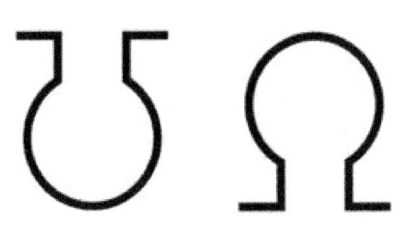

Game Called Life
Find and conquer <u>fear</u>
head on.

Extinguish fiery <u>anger</u>
in your blood.

Knock down a hard wall of <u>pride</u>.

<u>Accept</u> all that is.

Connects your dots to the stars
in <u>oneness</u>.

Red Prison
Paint a self portrait.
You love it.
It's all you care about.

Me, me, me, me.
Like an opera performance for one.

Self centered;
Trapped in illusion.

Secrets of Anger
"Not today. Some other way."

Bring change to what makes you angry.

Pin point the boiling point.

Caged;
Pacing lion
behind their eyes.

Raged.

Quite primal.
Plays its role in survival.

Sadness
Dehydrated by life.

I hurt.

In every face, it hides.
I see it in the world.

In myself.

Embarrassed

Dampen the biggest blow.
Reveal yourself before you are exposed.
We all do silly things, you know.

Into the spotlight.
Run toward pain.
It's just a chemical based game.

Your face lights up.
Red.
Sweat.
Get it over with quick,
it's for the best.

Be conscious of what you say.
You will break the loop one day.
Ignoring damage done
teaches in delay.

So get humiliated one thousand times
if you must.
You'll find every heart is pure
stardust.

Pride
Brick by brick
til you're sick, sick, sick.

You've built a wall
around no one left to fall.

You have so much to prove, standing so tall.
Deconstruct bricks that trap you in,
Mr. know it all.

Secret of Guilt
Search your heart.

Will you be able to heal?
Ignore a dead deal.

Consider yourself completely unconscious.
Confronted by an inner mirror;
Ignorance.
Consequences.
Rise above a guilty vibration before
you are crushed by your own kingdom.

Painful Loop
You say you don't feel that pain?

Stubborn fool,
too proud to admit.

Enjoy your scarring decisions
and the loop of it.

Forgiveness
The past has passed.
Though memory brings pain.
Forgive all those who have hurt you.
They're yet to wake up;
Insane.

Attraction
Compose your song into freedom.

Any colour you like.

Musical chords played into the universe.

She sings beautifully in return.

Secret of Laughter
As a child, I followed
my heart through laughter.
A natural medicine.

Open up and receive a secret.
Humour touches the heart
like a magnet.
Laughter filling a room
are the gifts of attraction.

Boundaries
My limits
must be broken.

Nothing keeps me behind
bars.

Already, I imagine them shattered
Shards of glass
scattered across the floor.

Detail for detail.
Another course I'll conquer.

Caged again,
but broken.

Keep them coming.

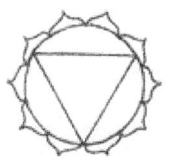

Funny Man
keep projecting humour, funny man.

Become the joke.

Life turns to comedy.
Ends in poetry.

A shift in reality.

Love and Fear
Tiny, upon a grain of sand
In my own mirror,
I stand.
I fear all I fail to understand.

Now,

love exists in all that I see.
I see myself in everything.

All I touch, taste,
hear, smell,
and think.

Reflection of me are
illusions and memory.

Secret of Love
You cannot give what you do not have.

Not until your deepest dive
would you understand
In your absolute;
Love.

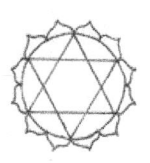

Passion
Poured into soul.
I can't take no for an answer.

What are the foundations of you?

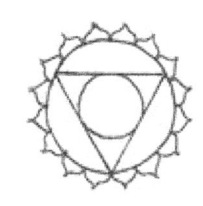

Project outward
For the whole world to see.
Deeper
and
deeper
passion gets to be.

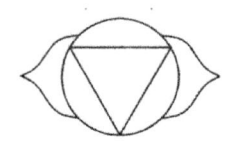

The "Art" In Heart
High vibrations in the square grooves.
Lose yourself in it.
Find yourself in it.
The canvas shows emotion.
Hold up your mirror of colors.
The reflection in the art is you.

Oneness/ connection
Inside our heart,
Death is transcendent.

Roots of the universe crack through the
glass dome of imagination
for the grand eye opening.

In the finite arena of stars,
births a shining bright light;
Consciousness.

"All is one"

Reflection/ mirror
In a mirrored dimension,
experience humiliation
to grasp humiliation.

Hate to receive hate.

Love to find love.

Heal to be healed.

Create to be created.

Chapter 5: Dimension

New Light
Reality, as never seen before.
Innocents, love and beauty
re-birthed into
infinity.

I see.

Step into the Realm
Brighter emptiness and colour
outside the rainbow.

You don't know
what you don't know.

Vanish through dimension three.
Into all you don't see.

Grab my hand
I'll pull you though new realms
of infinity.

Set yourself free.

Dimension of a Paintbrush
How do you see the paintbrush?

Wooden;
length, width and height.

There's more.

I see ways to make money.
I see tearing eyes.

History.
A way to change the world

All you *don't* see.

We overlook the
Dimensions of infinity.

Pocket
The universe exists in here.
In constant construction.
Soul introduction.
Reprogrammed to live without fear.

Hidden Dimensions
"This pain in my heart, it can't be filled.
No doctor needed, it will self heal.

I cry for attention but cannot be heard.
My heart takes its toll from physical words.

No family, nor friends can hear me now.
I'm the only one caught in this, somehow?

No sleeping,
nor eating, today or tomorrow
I've found all the time I could borrow.

A way out,
a new dimension;

Right in front of you
if you pay attention."

Past, Future and Present
Memory.
A vision.
Soak in the one and only existing moment.
In this infinite dimension.

The New Door
Desire,
accomplishment,
realization.

Emotional ingredients fuel your thoughts.
Intuition,
direction,
clarity.

Living dreams so tall.
Achieve it all.

Give it up.
Be rewarded once more
with your brand new
higher dimensional door.

Creation Hides
In the existing moment
In knowledge
In love

In the decision
In ignorance
In hate

In the dirt under your feet
In your strongest desires
And deepest sleep

Dismantle/ rebuild
Time
Height
Weight
Space
Possession
Separation
Meaning

No longer exists.
Dismantling the universe.

I am but mind,
putting meaning
to every illusion I find.

Sandbox
The multidimensional being
has fun in the sandbox
only for so long.

Shakes sand out of its pants when it's through.
Quickly wants out upon discovery.

Now
In this,
we experience the non physical.
Infinite possibilities of the imagination.
This moment of creation.

Unimaginable
It becomes more and more beautiful.

More than your mind can now handle.

Happening in the moment,
unable to process
death and existence;

Unimaginable.

The Unseen
Memory
Imagination
Perception

In this, we invent.
In this, we exist

Look passed physicality.
Into the new reality.

Imagine the Poem
Paint visuals that come to mind when you read this poem.
Don't forget the details.
Put down your brushes.
What did you paint?

Property less Pocket
As your eyes meet the page,
realize I *am* you.
Destined to meet the poem
and see the full truth.

A pocket with no properties,
I have no limit.
No doubt
And no problem creating.

Zip, zip!
In and out of the universe
I go.
The zipper pulls down and
The arena of stars
become a playground.

Zip zip!
Sneaking back into reality,
unseen.
Watch the universe
play out its new set of rules;
Enjoying the altered scenes.

Inside
Isness
Attachment
Physicality
Memory
Creation.

Higher realizations
within reach.
Here;
Now.

The Other Side
The creator paints a biased opinion.

We must experience all that is.
All that is not.
As everything.
As nothing.

Experience The Tree.
Falling and feeding;
tire swinging.
Drying and dying
multiplying.

Trapped in place; An eternity.
Water rises in the veins of each leaf.
Standing in soil and sand below me.

Eaten by bugs;
Hurting.

Lifetime planted.
Stillness and learning.
Observing.

From acorn to
stomachs
of animals,
to the dirt under
my feet,
worms and
sprouted saplings.
Droplets of rain
that soak the seed.
All who have
bitten the leaves.
And all who
breathe.

Mood

Inside the field,
emotions take over the room.

Feelings in shades of
greed, lust, envy.

I see in you,
colours of your truth.

Chapter 6: Existence

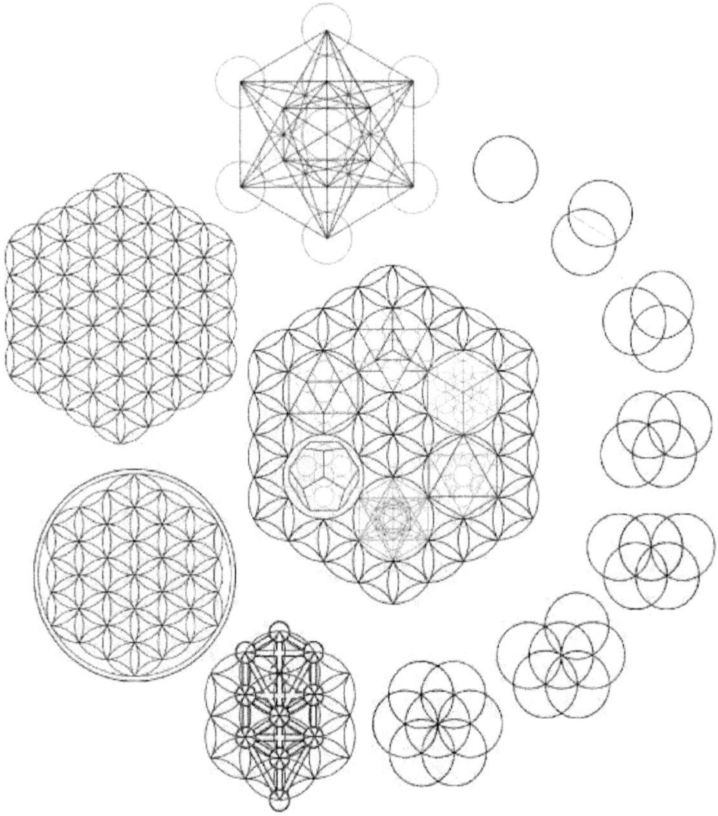

You Exist!
Wake up, you!
Everybody!
You are it!
Tell all the people!
You exist!
You exist!
Wake up from the illusions!

Centered
A small replica of the universe.
Brains branch out like a summer tree.
Sprouted from a centered seed.

Transmitting,
receiving
memory.

Entangled in light,
a self watering being.

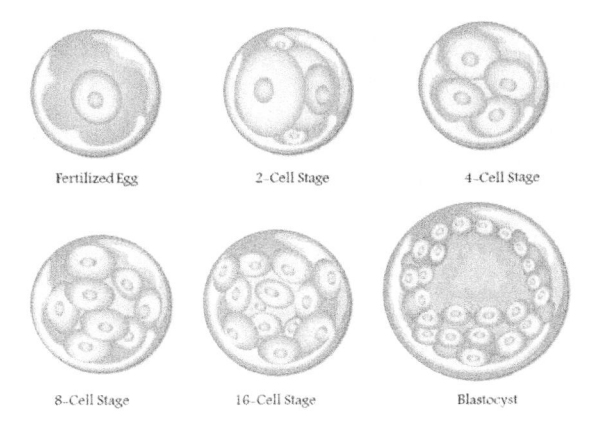

Fertilized Egg	2-Cell Stage	4-Cell Stage
8-Cell Stage	16-Cell Stage	Blastocyst

Fractal
Fire inside fire
Infinitely layered
Emotion
Truth
Atoms.
Deeper, deeper.
Fields inside a field.
Deeper, deeper.
Fractals of light in play.

Earth   Water   Fire   Air   Ether

Russian Tea Doll
Emotion
Thought
Universe
Element
Earth
Self

Hint
Everywhere you look,
hiding in plain sight,
hints are to be found.

Spinning galaxy in the sunflower.
Rock formations in the ground.

Patterns on the backs of animals;
In scales and fur.
Veins in leaves and rivers.

In clouds,
rain,
the human brain.
Reflections of soul and pain.

Life is warmth,
pressure and motion.
memory and imagination.

Energy Is
Energy lives.
Whirls and swirls
upon itself.

A universal mix.
Reconnecting consciousness.

As elements force movement,
they shift into beings.
Designed to be self perceiving.

In a recycling loop
of destruction and creation,
births conscious imagination.

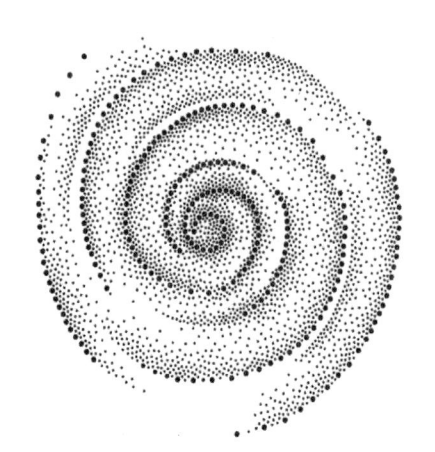

Snowflake
Her geometric structure is beautiful;
Symmetrical celestial
like galaxy stars.

Fractal shapes;
Radiation
like the sun
in an icy form

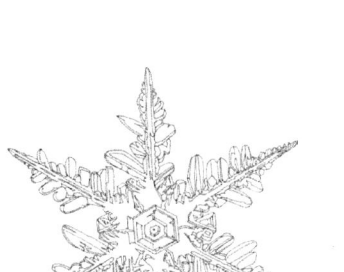

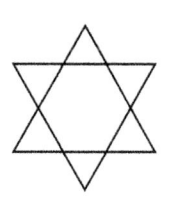

Spherical/ chemicals
All things that exists,
spherical.

Atoms.

On top of all you sit,
spherical.

Earth.

On top of all atop that is,
spherical.

Universe.

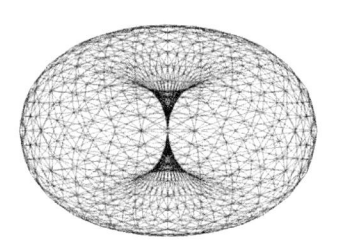

The Spiral Dynamic
Shells
Galaxies

Everywhere.

Draining into spiral.
Flowers
Eyes
Weather

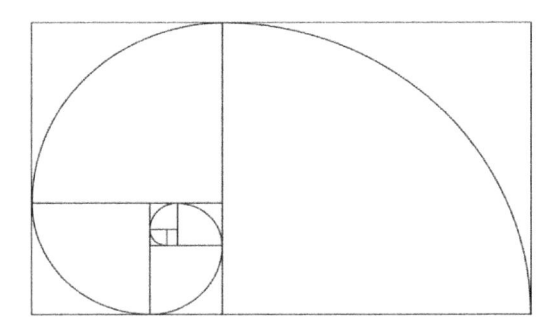

Motion
Heated and cooling is
pressure

Now on my walls and in my peripheral vision.
A repulsive magnetic movement.

All through space and earths' dirt,
we exist in patterns
of the universe.

Atom

What is there, is here
And here is there.
And this is the same as that.

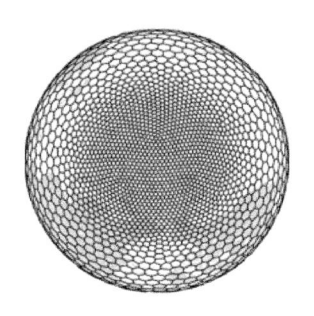

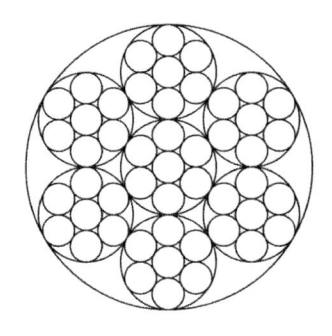

Field/ jar of marbles

Heat shuffles into white light and space we call
the sun, earth, planets and stars.

Like marbles condensed
in a self contained jar.

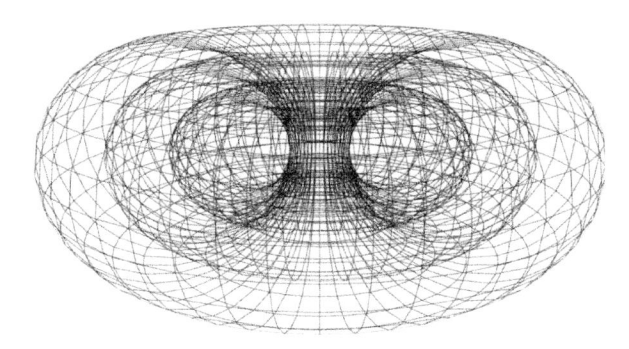

Radiation
All and none
atoms are one.
Pushed in every direction.
Light
that has always been.

I am the chosen.

Everything
Standing on atom, Earth
looking up at atom sun.

At night I see star atoms.
Under my feet, I see dirt atoms.
All that is black in between, no atoms.

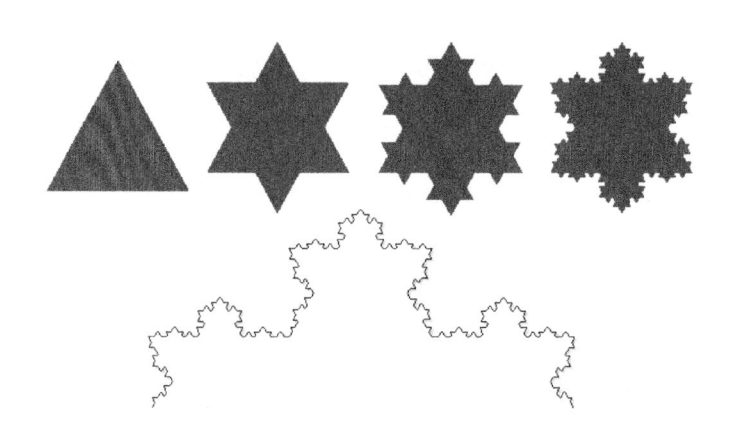

Space/Aether
Not any thing,
but holds structural meaning.
Space is not a thing.
No *thing*.
Nothing.

Black Hole/matter
A universe, twisting, breathing.
Black holes in everything.
Atom is the being.
Right in sight,
high in the sky,
as stars and anything
we see.

Sand/ stars
Slipping through fabric
of physicality.

Stars within stars
worlds within worlds,
space within space.

Forever searching.

Infinity in my peripherals,
swimming through galaxies
of hyrdrogen and metal
in a finite universe of self.

Elements
Always connected.
Elements are one.

Universal medium.

The cycle of light,
and
water we drink.

I am the mist,
Humidity.

Sound in perfect
symmetry.

From heat to cloud,
bolts of lightning
touching ground.

Space and Stars
What is more amazing?
The uncountable stars
or the space around them?

The observer?

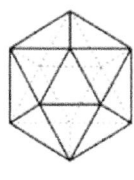

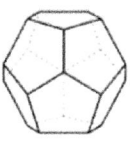

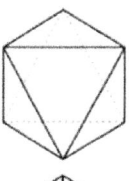

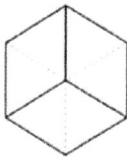

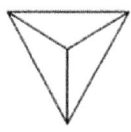

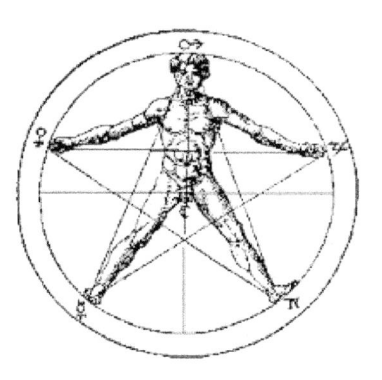

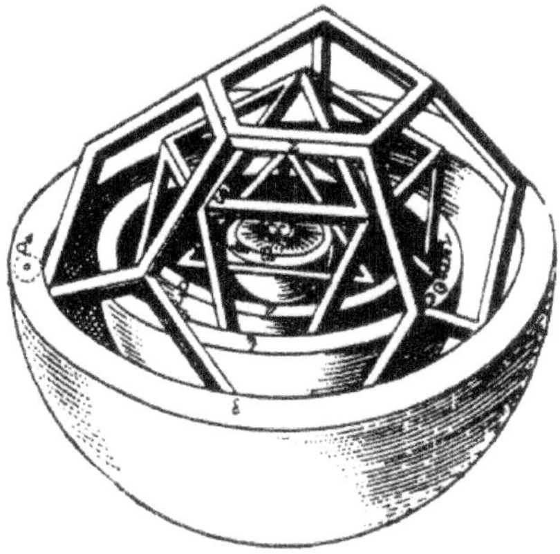

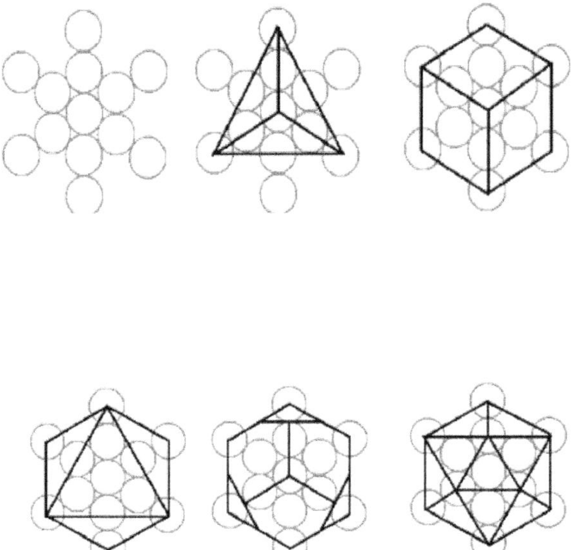

Gravity/ magnetism
Rocks accelerate when met in the air.
Repulsed.
Bubbles want out of water.
Repulsed.
The universe knows it's place
chemicals join themselves.

Trapped in and around nothingness.
It is the warmth of something-ness.

Infinity, atoms go on
in a sphere.
Dancing   rainbow   in
layers.

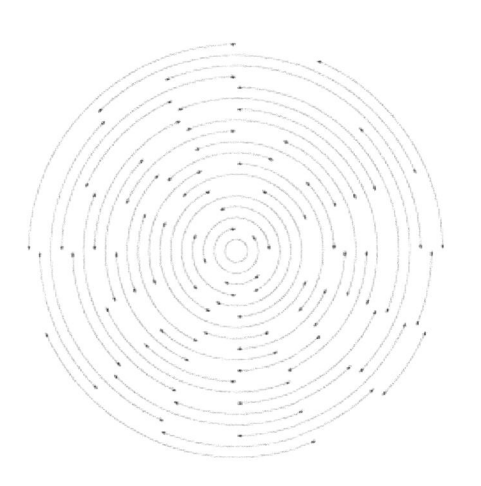

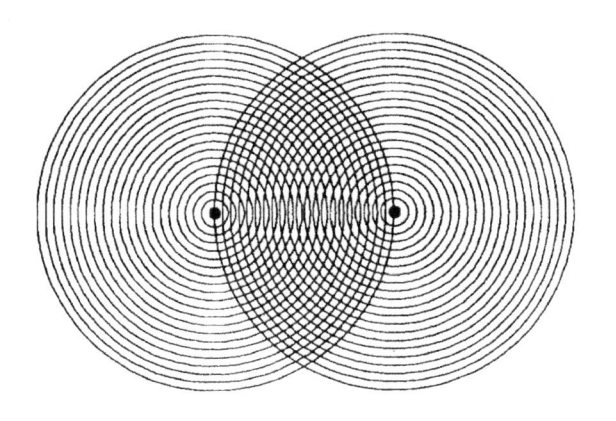

Everything You See
There is no darkness,
but all light
in all that holds heat.

Everything you see
exists in a three dimensional reality.

Heat, Pressure, Consciousness
Energy is the radiating universe.
Field
Force
Flame in repulsion.
Never ending.
Forever burning.

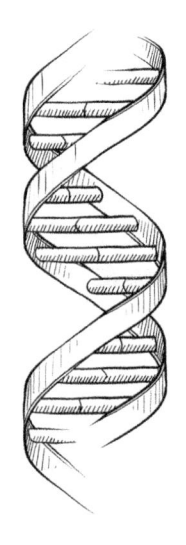

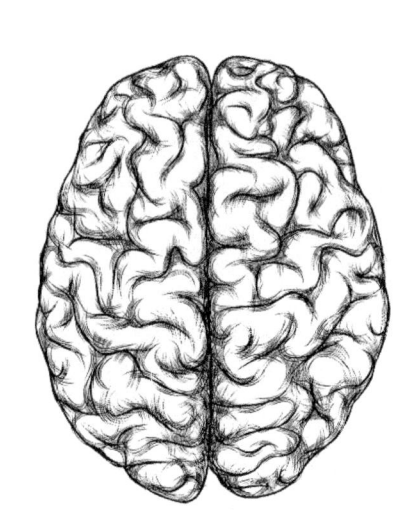

Cosmic Seed
It has no name.
All bodies the same.

Yet to wake.
I am give and take.

Born in darkness and greed.
Life.
Who are we, indeed?
But a self watering
Seed.

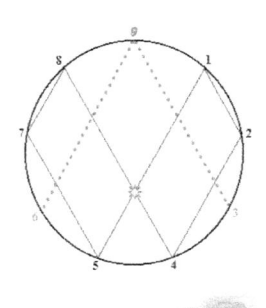

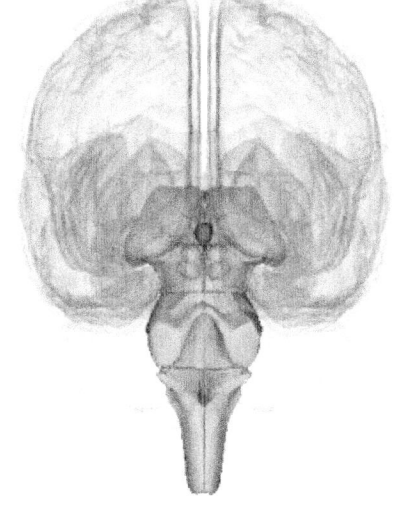

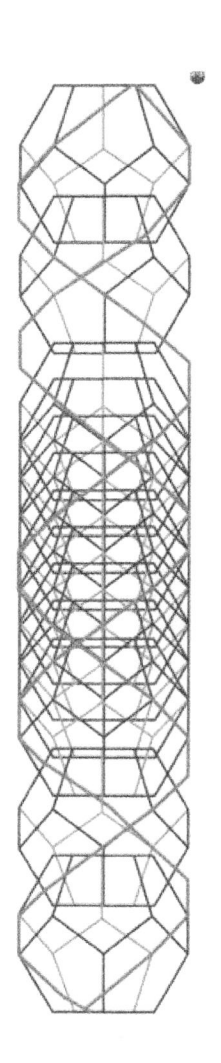

Rain/water
Scattered information.
Rain clouds swoop in on my command.
Nearly drowning in the discovery.
Absorbs in my pores;
Memory.

She has been
calling all these years
and I've known this.
Revealing herself,
she comes out from hiding behind the curtains of reality.
Dancing her way in; Hip-fully.

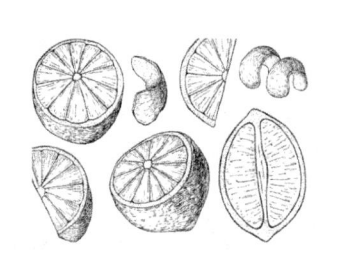

Toroidal Fruit
Oranges
grapefruit;
Take shape of the universe
lemon
lime;
Loop of life
grapes
apples
kiwi
coconut.
In the middle, creation

Mighty Trees
An acorn is packed so tight,
it is difficult
to believe
they grow into such
mighty beings.

All packed with potential
to become
these mighty things.

And with this mighty life,
it allows mighty me.

Trading breath with the
mighty brilliance
of these mighty trees.

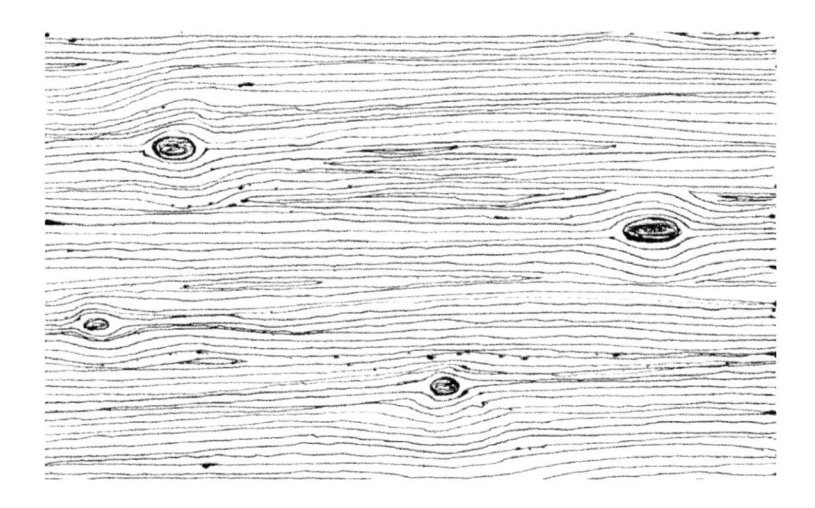

Circuit Board sky
Sparks going off
in the mind
for the idea that is life.
All stars connect like
lightening striking flame
That heats Earth, the bulb.

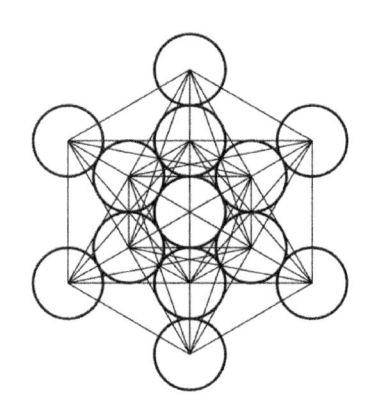

Earth
My song and vibration.
It is my name.
My lesson.
A canvas,
A playground.

Rainbow/ magnetic
Inside   earth,   a
rainbow
of layers.
Molten heat
Cooling rocks
Life
Atmosphere
Space

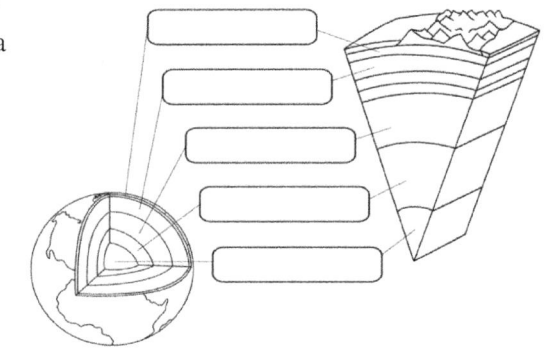

Connect by temperature,
a colorful linking universe.

Dancing Planets/ excited atoms/ chemical reaction
In perfect symmetry,
the universe dances.
She is all shapes.

Vibration.

Thought and action.
Repulsed by all that she is not.
Reason for existence.
The magic of the magnetic mind.

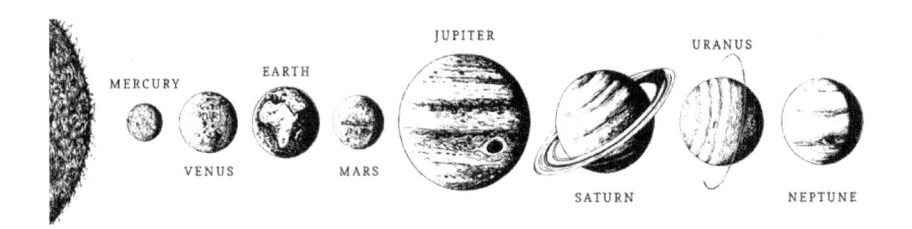

White/ inside the ether
I know you're in there and I know you know I
know of your existence.
You wait for us to discover the center.
Center of the moon.
Center of Sun, and Earth.
The center of every atom.
Space.

Silver/ metal
Dense metals expand like a balloon.
Inside the iron dome,
Space, planets and life.
Like a mirror, reflection.
Heated and cooled,
down to the shiny core.
Iron is the center
of the universe.

Welding,
melting
molten
magnetic
metals.

Burning, burning.
Creating space.

Light
Creation, itself.
Consciousness.
At the center of all, a blinding light
that is the mind and being.
Potentially anything.

Red/ core/root
Lava, blood.
Heat in the core of our
existence.
Heart, Earth;
Pumping universe.
Radiating
cries and Pain.
Iron that boils
in our veins.

Orange/outer core
Over and over
sprouting up from
core to surface.

The crust is cooler.
Rusty, rocky clay
in hot, dense dirt.

Yellow/mantle
Rubble of a lighter colour.
Gas, smelly sulfur.
sands are the crust
touching surface.

Green/life
Blue skies above.
Soil below the being.
Frequencies in between
are shades of green

In the center of the rainbow,
life is the colour of existence.

Springing up,
trees, grass
Bamboo.

In the centered pocket,
Earth.

Blue/self
Water, air.
With the right words,
say what you must
to the elements of ourselves.
See what cant be seen.
Speak your truth into the reflecting
being.

Indigo/consciousness
Beyond the sky
set a course for the unseen.
The other side, darkness.
As me.

Violet/ wisdom
Tears fall down all
the beautiful beings.
I see with clarity,
transparent beauty.
Truth of self
outside the body.

Black/emptiness
Nothingness,
potential
to be;
Everything.

Seen in the depths of space
the eye;
Beholder of beauty.

Between fractals of all things,
the mind watches;
Imagines matter
and meaning.

Gold
Healing,
conductive;
It can be consumed.

For purity,
killed over star dust,
fought to our doom.

Proof of the penetrated
mind.
Wear the colour that's
hard to find.

Worn as royalty.

Notice me.

Colour/ imagination
In the infinite flame,
sparks, suns
fire.

Shades of your choice
interpret meaning
of your desire.

In this big picture,
Stardust is all we see.

Radiating warmth in all colours.
So stand back, what does it mean?

Meaning of Meaning
The meaning of meaning
does not exist until you realize the
meaning of meaning does not exist.

Colours and Sound
The truth we believe is simply
illusions of meaning.

The big picture we're looking for
is the being we're seeing.

Collecting favorites;
Stars shine in every colour.

Call them decorations.

Stars in the shape of
tables,
chairs,
and all forms of desire.

Colour and sounds;
   What you choose to be around.

If You Back Up Far Enough
Continuously,
I believe I stepped
out of the loop.
Travel to the
another time
through cosmic
soup.

Taking back with
me,
all the knowledge I
can carry.
Backing up far
enough
to see something
scary.

Stars draw in the
infinite being.
It stands back
to interpret
meaning.
And it was itself
it was imagining.

Being
Distant stars,
dots on your face.
She is nature;
Resembles earths surface.
Walks with
lightning strikes
in her veins.
Black hole in each eye.
Pulsing heart, core of heat.
The universes medium
that pumps and breathes.

Lungs, like roots of a tree.
Brain shaped like clouds
filled with memory.

Streams of water run down your cheek
like rivers, vines
streams and creeks.

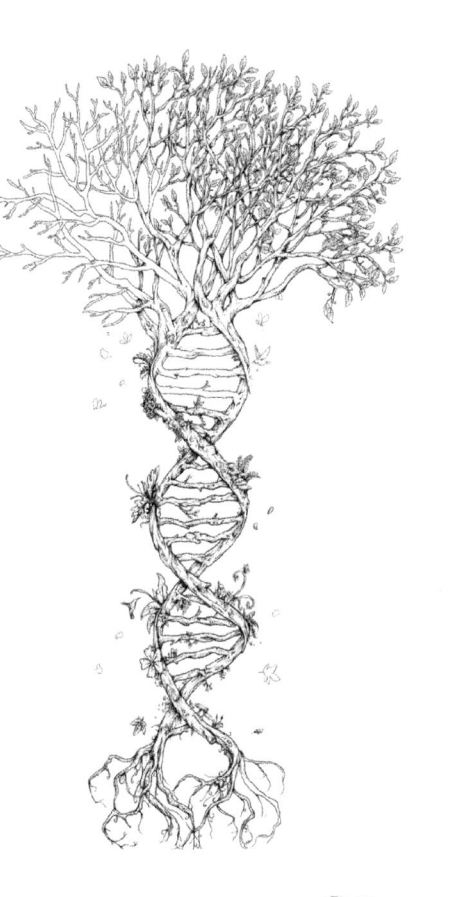

Breathing/dying
Save your being
from the oven
that is alchemy.

Breathe slowly.

Make your last breathe
your dying wish.
The rotting heat is a
pulsing beat of existence

Burning
Fulfilling every wish,
unbiased.
All are granted.

Over the horizon,
the eye climbed.

People soaking in heat of greed.

Scorching down on the towns.
Watching earth closely
as we burn away our being.

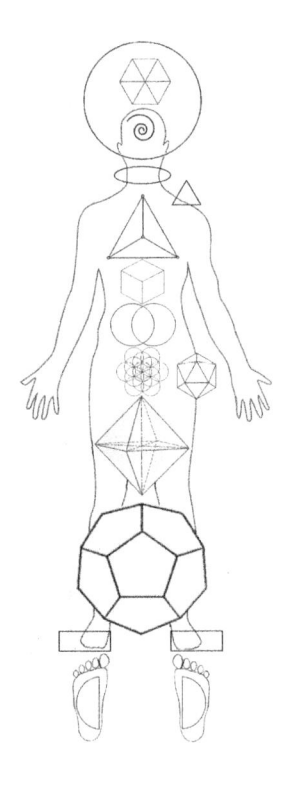

Outside the Pattern/Locusts
Perfect patterns persist.
We must have perfection to exist.

Locusts eat who step foot out of line.
Through trial, error and death.
Nature gets no rest.
For the body to work as a whole.
To take any structure at all.

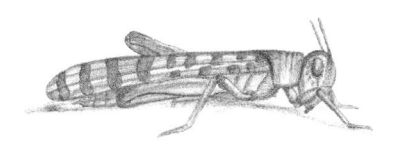

Matter and Mind/ thought
Collecting your stars in a row.
Inhale, exhale.
Take time on this idea.
Think in precision,
down to detail,
your solution.

Singularity
Through pain, a beautiful experience arises.
You are the singularity.
The one truth.
Existence.

Blood
Flowing, flowing.
Blood creates
monsters,
mirrors, illusions,
and angels.

Iron
Sisters of blood;
brothers of war.
Reek of forbidden spilled metals.

Iron flows through the veins
of us all.
We are the fight,
and light of the world.
Still a distant, dim lit star;.

              Fire
I've watched the universe
burn.
Again and again.
I can never take my eyes off it.

Action
Proof of truth,
projected.
Out and perceived.

Be dealt the sequences.
Whatever you receive.

On a true decision, reality is created.
Yesterday, tomorrow, now,
energy is traded.

Desire
Forever lost in illusion.
The burning core of the universe;
desire.
Continuously searching.
Eternally chanting to
find meaning in it all.

Temporarily satisfied.
Forever driven.

Take Your Pick
Knowledge, but desire;
Or
Ignorance, but fulfillment.
Ultimate ultimatum
as human.
As spirit;
And God

Becoming
I've taken 99% of the universe out
of the equation.
Pressure, heat, perception
is what stands.
What does it matter?

If you ever realize consciousness,
you've become everything.
 Planets, space
the universe,
everyone.
In search of yourself
and none of it would matter.

Curse
Now that you know,
it becomes prisoner.

Again and again.

Freed for many years.

Sleep and ignorance
Until now.

I'm sorry to have woken you.

This torture
warps a brain,
but existence is being awake for the pain.
In divine order of infinitely awakening.

Existing
We are not just living in the moment.
We're trapped in the moment.
We are the moment.
Now.

Layers of God
Mirrors of earth
stare deep
into the universe.

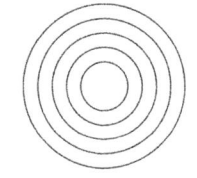

Nothingness;
I recognize myself as
the light of god,
Burning away the layers of god
to find itself.

Birth
Coming into existence
differently each time.
From the womb,

now the mind.

Telepathy
One day, words wont be needed.
Truth being the only answer.
Not needed to be communicated.
The obvious, eliminated.

Chapter 7: Reality

Evolution

In <u>fear</u>,
<u>anger</u> finds a desperate way out, but at what cost?
New powerful knowledge swims through boiling veins.
Flames so high,
it sets you free of your worst nightmares.
But find yourself in yet
another pickle.
Fight becomes the only answer.
Persuade me that you aren't angry.
Self control becomes the enemy.

<u>Pride</u>, the entity that allows no growth.
With it,
evolution moves slow.
In time, brick by brick
The wall is lowered

Now ready for truth.

<u>Acceptance</u> of itself
deep down,
for humanity, and
for all.
Discover attraction
Discover vibration.
One after another, unlocking the higher self.
Mind is a library of secrets.

Like a shining star, becoming the light of the world.
Peeking into hidden dimension. <u>Oneness.</u>

Outer Mirror
Belief is reality.
Earth;
My outer mirror.

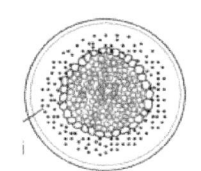

Chemical experience
Decision
Reaction
Experience

What you are experiencing
is a brain chemical reaction.

What we have called for so long,
the human experience.

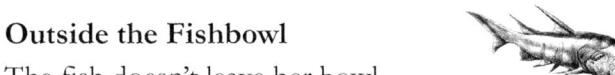

Outside the Fishbowl
The fish doesn't leave her bowl.
She's yet to find her soul.
No desire to find more.
Yet to notice her
higher dimensional door.

Scavenger Hunt
The game begins.
Who finds themselves, wins.

What you call life,
is a scavenger hunt for
knowledge and
Experience.

Discover yourself
in new light.

The hints lie in others and deep within.
Replaying a game of chess,
gather the pieces and play again.
Truth is at the end.

What We Call Reality
Every vibration
interacts with creation.
What we call reality
is a looping imagination.

Ape Man
This one punches and slaps the mirror.
No self discovery and
lives in fear.

No intention to understand.
Take a look at yourself, ape man.

Unorganized
Lets paint something beautiful for ourselves.

First, lay down your colours.
Now primer the paint.

Apply the canvas.
Now get out your brush...

Backwards!
Backwards!
Backwards!
Everything so far
has been backwards!

Unconscious
Insanity.
Over and over.
Ignorance.
Over and over.
Unconscious.

Trying to Evolve
Are you trying to evolve?
How could this all be solved?
Who's faulted and flawed?
Who all is trying to evolve?

Mirror
The present moment is reflection.
How do you look?
How conscious can one be?
Patterns all around;
Some may be keys.
Your conscious projection
is reality

Poisoned
What is consumed
is what it becomes.
Water,
air,
food.
Tricked into illness
Toxic vibrations.
The mind has been poisoned.

Sick and Tired
Too sick to care.
Darn tired, but to be fair,
not enough to learn this lesson;
Or the pain wouldn't be there.

Deciding I am done
being sick and tired
sets me free.

Creation from the Outside
The mind observes.
Chooses what to believe.
Wants nice things
for others to see.

"It will impress them greatly, and I'm well groomed"

The false mind, impressed, and consumed.

Creation of perspective has got you again.
You keep forgetting who you are, friend.

Puppets
Controlled;
Exposed to illusion.
Reality bends to the will.
Each believe their reality
to be real.

Wooden beings
under spells of pulled strings.
People of earth, dance out of rhythm.
Wanting more and more
meaningless things.

Fool
Fools, fools!
What is it?
Scratching your head as you try
grasping the reality in front of you.
Tip of the tongue
You're all fools!
But I, the biggest one.

Virus
Life destroying life.
It takes over.
Pain inflicting entity.
Poison in all you touch.
inside and out, you are
hurting, thriving,
soon dying.

Hunters
We've become hunters
trapped
behind invisible bars.
Now mad men,
Speaker of spells
praising mars,
doing harm.
Not yet realizing
we are stars.

Sickness
Sickness and anger go hand in hand.
Stress kills a man.

Like a car, blood is the oil;
Keep it clean,
or will run like an old machine.

Negativity obscures the mind.
Thoughts pays a heavy fine.

Unbalanced
Consumption,
assumption.

Unbalanced,
missing pieces.

Unconscious.
It has built the belief of medicine.
Stolen the belief of creation.

Blood Pressure
This moment causes me discomfort.
Blood boiling.
Rising temperature.
I feel a disturbance in my heart.
Depression is the setting loop.

Stop the Pain!
No more!
No more pain is necessary.
Imagination is an incredible
thing.
We're insane!
We're insane!

Unsteady Hand
Shaking and shaking

Slip
Cut

Your hand bleeds.
Intellect slices itself
if blood is what it needs.

Blame
If anything, we can call it ignorance.
Among the galactic, who knows who,
laugh
as we live life like a comedy skit.
Blaming god for our existence.

Cotton and Linen
The ill mind pulls the trigger.

Does cotton kill a man?
Does Linen do one in?

You can collect a handful, but grasp the pattern
and watch a mind change on a dime.

Fools Gold
Fool, fool cosmic drool.
Chasing gold.

Selfish, selfish fool,
you *are* the gold.

With all you hold,
watch life unfold
and behold;
Your soul is sold.

Not Yet In Harmony
Emotion is the vibration.
Striving to sing the same notes.
We are not yet in harmony.
Illusions of separation creates a sour chord.

Loops
Scars on your skin,
in your heart,
unable to be forgiven.
Mistakes and ignorance, visible to the world.

What did you do to earn that badge?

Are we willing to show them?
Grow from them?

Ignorance
Ask the biggest question you can imagine.
Deeper
Deeper
Deeper
Without an answer, what are we doing?

Missing the Point
Impossible to be heard,
I speak no longer words.

Tell a child,
"You'll be in love one day."

"No way!"
is what he'll say.

Tell the prideful,
"The kingdom is the heart.
We are NOT apart."

He didn't know where to start...

They nailed him dead.
Completely missing the point, instead.

Stalemate
The sane are seen insane
and insane seem the same

Cannot Be Heard
No matter how loud.
No matter the arrangement
of words,
we have walked a different path.
Our universes clash.
Meet me in middle ground
and dance to anagreeing sound.

The Dog Tilts Its Head
Though shown one thousand times,
can't seem to find the nob.
Inches from our face,
the universe
looks us dead in the eye.
We tilt our heads as well.

Different Frequency
Oneness.
Fear.
The insane recognize the mirror
as insanity.
Not yet heard by all humanity.

Can you hear me so far?

Static between radio stations,
hiss.

Raise to my vibration.

Volume is no factor.
You must <u>truly</u> be existing to see.

Hear,
feel,
experience me.

Attacking the Mirror
I complain people around me
do not understand
the discovery.

Angered by the pain.
It is me again
attacking the mirror.
I am the ape in fear.

Drained
Drilling, drilling
Spilling, spilling
blood and oils.
Fighting, stealing
depleting ourselves
mentally, physically

Anxiety
Peal back the layers of reality as you see.
It's not all its cracked up to be.

Take apart the world
piece by piece.

Reality has become a disease.

Suffering.
The world fights you,
frightens you.
Driving chemicals will
break through.
Take the step further, nervous one.
Oddities in your circles.

Mind games and deception
upon earth's reflection.
Any questions?
Now is the time
to make your move.
Your choice is perfection.

Slave to the Mind
Slaves never realize themselves as slaves.
Animals raised in a cage
have nothing beyond the bars to break.

Social Construct
Created by mind
built by consciousness.

Tables, chairs,
your name
and being.

Height, weight
time, death and other
material things.

You Only Want Freedom
You want your money.
You need a little more time.

Escape the illusions of today
and you will find

your freedom.

Get your head together.
Put your mind at ease.

Your brain will click and it will stick
now see...

you only want freedom.

Alternate You
Anything you wish to be.
Another existence lies within reach.

Let it be truth
and it will be you.
Any dream of your choosing.

Illusions!
In a heavy storm
a poet knocks down the front door.
Speaks of a disastrous downpour.
All the towns people put away their forks.

Everything is an illusion

The people

Me.

Truth or Poison
Tell the truth or be poisoned.
What is consumed, believed, and said comes true.
Unconscious,
in its toxic surroundings.

Three Dimensional Prison
Call it hell if you want.
I am trapped in a newly realized realm.

All Seeing Eye
It takes the eye of God
to see the reality
in front of you.
Hidden deep
in the continuity of illusion.

Pieces
Some have collected parts of the puzzle.
Some have yet to realize the puzzle.
Some deny the puzzle.
Some deny denying the puzzle.

Integrity
The galaxy quiets down
as I put on a show for them all.

The eye of living
watches closely to see your next shot a nature.
Your next escaping move.

Judged by your vibration.
Voice and dance groove.

Roped into the Illusion
Anything and anyone who crosses my path
will be trapped.
You *are* my mind.
The necessary piece to break free.
Each hold peices of me.

Disbelief
Maybe not yet, do you believe,
but reality is yours.

The universe is yours.

All that is, is yours.

Have a look around.
Admire your art.
It shined so beautifully
that it has blinded you
into disbelief.

Attachment
Bound by matter,
soul is confused.
What should I do.
Who is who.
Attached.
It insists on sewing
emotion to a material world.

He thinks he's a car.
She thinks She's money.

What We Call Time
Set the clock that
counts down your days till death.

Count the times
gone around the sun.

Nothing but a collection of numbers for fun.

Every second reminds me
of a pointless existence.
I'm never looking at that clock again.

Live forever
in absolute truth.

This moment right here.
Slows, speeds;
Ceases to exist
in the mind of
you.

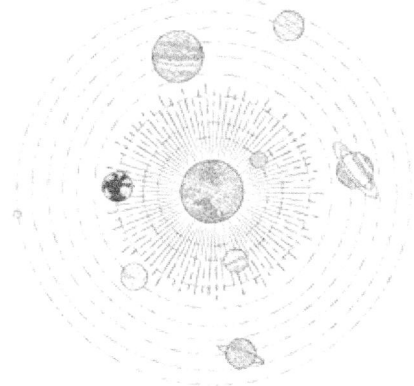

Rotting
Tick tock.
Your body will rot.

Flesh falls from the bone.
How many lessons can you learn in this form?

Appreciate the decay.
Life works that way.

Reality so swiftly moves.
Caught in the universes groove.

The body will one day be removed.

Timeless
Today feels like next week.
Yesterday feels like now.
An eternity.
All those years lived in a moment.
20 years feels like the last hour.
and tomorrow never comes.

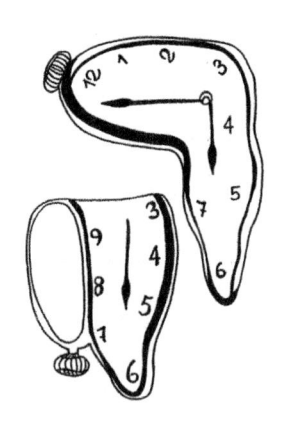

Living
Always in thought,
I cannot concentrate on any
other existence.

Leaks in the roof,
holes in the floor.

Out here
for what feels lifetimes, or more.
I've experienced loss,
freedom, love
heartache, detachment
silence and God.

As time goes by,
I am closer;
wiser.

Nature claims my home.
But still, this life is beauty.

All life; beauty.

The Play/ the world is a stage/ role
Which role are you playing?
The main character, if I may.
Don't laugh at me, okay?
I hope I don't fall off stage!
What would the people say?
With broken bones, I would lay.
It would haunt me
every day.

Performance
Laughter and sadness.
The only truth.

All else, a performance,
preference,
illusion.

Judge
Dare to wear a suit
in this game of experience.
Be timed by your sitting,
judged by your unbuttoning.

Colour
Size
Tie
Choice in drink
is your identity they think.

Separation
I keep getting fooled by the illusion.

If I beg for mercy, who would hear me?

I'm me, but not this me.
I'm all, but not this body.

Nobody.
Everybody;
Everything.

Fooled Again
Freedom only lasts
As long as it takes to realize the bars.

In stages, freedom comes and goes.
Always to find yourself in a prison
with desire and the fire to break free.

Life; The Grand Illusion
The first years of your life will be your absolute
truth.
Whatever they tell you will be.
Your surroundings,
programmed until the soul breaks free.

In this realm, outside the illusion,
we live forever
In our desires, an eternity

Out the Window
Trying to understand my mind.
Notes piled high around the room.
Everything I know, gone
out the window.
But still,
rings in my heart as true.

Forever Young
Looking back, you were
just a kid.
Stubborn, but
growing.
Forever in trial and error
of ignorance
Never Grasping the full truth.

Shift
Higher dimensions lie within every human.

Prove yourself divine and
equal to the rest.

Dance circles around your
creation.
Put reality to the test.

In happiness;
Sadness;
Life-ness.

Escape
Earthly obstacles.
Built for you,
by you.

Learn to Learn
The secret is to
blow your mind to pieces and question reality.
The mundane becomes extraordinary.

Another door opens.
Traced back to your existence.
Find in every direction,
the radiation of passion.

Understanding
My body changes
when I say the right words.
See the right things.
Be the right me.

Moving in the direction my heart pulls.
My skin tingles and breathes
as this truth enters my being.

The Steepest Obstacle
Admit you know nothing
so we can begin to learn.

If you could only realize
the existence of you,
you would have then
climbed the steepest obstical.

Throw out the old
perspective.
Make room for something bigger.

Trading Energy
Note for note,
frame by frame.

It sees itself as
One and the same.
In this universe, you get out what you put down.

What is perceived
can now be received
quicker
for next time around.

Making an Entrance/ raising vibration
Steal the room.
Reality as water
taking shape to your hand.

Sweep the people with comedy.
Outshining even
the toughest man.

Trade For Something Higher
Give up material items to experience non physicality.
Uncover what you don't see.
Give up the thought of this life;
Experience purpose.
Give up all that you thought was true.
Discover belief within you.

Set of Tools/ gratitude
Forgiveness is a scythe to
hack away vines that hide the trail.

Gratitude digs up the roots.

Be thankful why the vines hid the Pathway for so long.

Healed in Return
Alleviate guilt in others.
They may set you free.
Forgive those yet to understand reality.

Mind needs healing.
We have been unconscious;
And killing.

Delay/ inner child
I wont call this time travel;
Not really.
Lets call it a delayed reaction.

Use these poems to pass through.

In your mind,
travel back to a time
Give your inner child this truth.

Prisoner of Words
That with no name;
Contained.
"I cant,
I wish,
no choice"
All assumed,
all I say aloud.
All that I put meaning
has trapped me
In my own words

Fine Lines
More and more,
the line is thinning.

Often crossed
Completely unseen.

Words used favourably
is the hurting being.
Biased actions,
slow awakening.

Receiving Vibrations
Highs or lows

I love you
I hate you

Push and pull.
Words vibrate to
the center of your skull.

Say the Right Words
Searching for the perfect words.
What is the sound that brings us
together?
Meet me as a medium of wisdom.
Have with me,
unbiased conversation.

Every Vibration
Like a chain reaction,
change starts within.
Whips back around again.
                Truth,
        Knowledge,
Evolution.
It waits for us all.

Emotional
Humidity in the air.
Attached by breath.

Projects emotion;
Injects a notion.

We've enchanted the moisture
In the sky and plants.

Water has turned to blood.

Entrusted with language,
emotions are in the molecules
And vibrating pockets of air.

Unbiased
How do you feel about an unbiased poem?

Bad Vibration/ stung
I would question our being
back to the beginning,
if ever stung by a bee.

I stand purely;
unbiased,
honestly.

Overwhelming
Place words into poetry
in order of importance.

Put to paper all that is true.
Do not let the universe overwhelm you.

You'll find it to be only one word.
The most beautiful poem you ever heard.

Unity
This
us-ness,
this
life-ness,
this
Oneness.
What do I call this?

I'm at a loss for words.
So much beauty.

Meet You on the Path
I can see your past,
present, and future.

In your health, the way you live,
your slouching back.

Attitude
and sadness.

My gift is to remind you
it was meant to be this way.
You are the perfect being.
Beyond kings and queens.
These are the lessons we must learn.

Divine order takes a course
like chapters
in a story book.

You're the star.

Emotions in the Mirror
Happiness and love.
Anger and fear.

Release energy
like magic words in a mirror.

Receive your creation.
How does it make you feel?

Reflection revealed?

Perspective
What is real to me
may be different to you.
We've walked a different path
what we believe to be truth.

Now coming to agree.
We share the same journey
as crossing light of certainty

Passing Moment/opportunity
Opportunities are only there
if you recognize it as one.
Others call it a passing moment.

Somewhere in the room
lies a dimension.
Change.
Can you see the future?
A fork in the road.

Are you conscious enough
to see the hard turn of reality?

Too Far Gone
My mind is too far gone
for the game you're playing.

And believe me,
it is pain
to no longer care what you are saying.

It's something I'm hating,
but debating on staying
in the presents of someone
insane.

Self Control
All that I want, is me.
I control all that I see
and what I wish to be.

If You Could Hear Me
Inspirational
Unstoppable
Unimaginable
Multidimensonal

Allow these vibrations into your being.

Say them,
or sing.

You would become magical, it would seem.

The Turning Point
Many paths to choose from.
All leading to the same goal.
Knowledge is your reward.
Even if you don't decide,
Your reality is created.
Only you create this experience.
Understand
Reality.
Don't think too hard,
Every part of the path is
Consciousness leading to the
Infinite
Subconscious intake.
In the very instant of decision,
Our reality changes if we can
Numb the fear.

Multidimensional
Ripped to confetti,
I find me;
My soul.

A raging passion, freed.

I am water,
The Fish
and bowl.

Celebrating Freedom
Long strands of hair;

Down to your ankles, freedom is showing.

Nakedness and purity.

Nature is giving.

The sun shines on all that I am.

In my freedom,
no longer hiding.

Look.
This is my truth.

Helpful Modern Recipe For Life
Money- Buys time
Time- Spend on yourself
Self- Discovery
Death- Dissolves illusions

Nature's Jacket
No longer must I look where I go.
Nature throws it's jacket
over every puddle.

Tingling
There's a static flow
in the body.

Never leading to something bad.
I never say no.

Life happens
In this moment;

Never letting go.

If You Can Picture It/ earthy matter
Distractions everywhere.
Vow to focus to completion
until the dream is no longer a dream.
The picture appears.
Be it love or hate,
passion turns to matter.

Whatever You Want
Focus on this one goal.

We have a choice to be consumed
or inspired.

Tune into happiness.
You become that.

Vibrate on frequencies of your wishes
You become that.

We can do anything.
In your control, you set the rule.

In your universe,
you can do it all.
Get wild,
get passionate.
It will happen

Desire materializes.
This is your dream.

As Real As You Make It
I understand the illusion that I am.
I feel that all is real,
but I know the truth.
Reality is as real as you make it.

Too Incredible
I wouldn't be surprised if you
don't hear me at this time.

It's too beautiful
Too fantastic
Too terrifying to accept
Too good to be true

Transparent Bridge
In a realm of illusion,
a bridge is held up by belief.

What a drop;
Surely to your death.

Driven by desire to cross.

Without doubt, already,
they see themselves
on the other side.

Bending Space and Time
For you, galaxies watch
to see your next trick.

No Rules

In the fabric of reality,
punch holes.

Reach out and touch another being.
There aren't any rules.
We can do anything.

In your mind,
be true.
No limits at all.
There is no universe without you.

Stop the clock
or live forever in debt.
If it can't be done
it was never meant.

Check Mate

No match for me.
I've got this game won.

No longer just
behind the board.

In your mind;
I predict your next move.
I play alone.

The New Human
Aligned with nature,
silence finds a conscious.
Every questions ever asked, answered
in its deepest truths.

Different light shines on a dim lit marble.

The new human
walks the illuminating path of earth.
Finds a way to be heard.
Carries no weapon
or word.

Fine Tuning
Set aside
what no longer guides you.

Shed attachments;

Material,
emotion.
Now it is time to pick your battles;
Your heaven.

Love,
knowledge
and laughter.

Enjoy Life/ all that you love
From this point on,
enjoy life in any state of mind.
As long as you wish.
Enjoy all you create and dismiss.

Discover
Learn
Become.

All that you are;
All that you love.

With You At All Times
There is a place you could
go to obtain knowledge necessary to your every
wish.

How will you use it?

Some wont realize it.
Some would lock themselves inside;
Barricade the door and make sense of reality.

Records
Imagine infinite knowledge
No limit whatsoever.
Truths upon truths,
Every being adds to the collection;
Replicating the one infinite mind.
Nothing out of grasp for the
Eternal multi dimensional being;
Through lifetimes of memory.

Handed Down Knowledge
Music.
Cave art and language.
Poetry, stone structure.
Tablets set in clay.
Books.
In this moment,
we have them at our hip.

Let's Go/ wake up
What is it going to take?
Here is my vibration to you.
That's all I can do.

Wake up
Wake up

Really, it's time.
Grab your four dimensional keys and lets head out of this thee dimensional world.

The Art of Art
Caught in thought
A self reflection.

Exploring every new door in this direction.

Throughout the mind,
Heartache and
Pain.

Push it firmly
Into the paint.

Hand Picked
As life I served
I get what I deserve.
All that I love and earn.
Delivered by the universe.

Infinity In Your Eyes
They smile at me in a way
that they know I know.
I smile back and saw in their crows feet
that they knew I know they knew I know.
And in that moment, sharing a glimpse
of infinity.
Nodding at eye level in agreement.

Memory
Stumbling into something familiar.
These sounds;
They are me.
I play this instrument.
Right where I left off on my journey

Past Lives
I see your path;
One I no longer wish to repeat.
In you, I see the old me;
And in those I no longer wish to be.

Alignment
Intelligence aligns itself.
Physical form to plant its roots.

Starting with the decision,
The foot of god is sewn.

Seeded with secrets found in the soil;
Becoming conscious of it's existence

Higher Intelligence
You can't see it;
You're busy indulging.
Look at "I" as a product of the universe.
Just one.

I am the black hole in the skies.
See them in my eyes?
Indulgence of space.
god.
This body is proof.
The old truth shatters.
Nothing else matters.

Unfolding Lotus
This need for truth is the path of beauty;
Rooted deep.
Life unfolds in stages.
Flowers emerge from the mud;
Bloom
into something
equal to God.

At peace;
In creation with nature.
On a thrown of its own kingdom.

Obsidian
The mirror has broken.
Freed from attachment;
Freed from ourselves.
The rope slips around
and off of my neck.
Freed from the noose
Freed from ignorance.
In the ways of recent behaving.
Freed of the illusion
that a mirror could be
enslaving.

Witches And Wizards

Young, old,
ugliness and beauty.
Say it allowed, in your truth,
and so it shall be.

A war of magic, witches are here.
Wizards never left, We've only disappeared.
Still walking among you
in your disbelief and fear.

We think we are human
but under old casted spells.
Forbidden curses
upon ourselves

Young magician,
you are now only waking.
We are the witches and wizards
causing the greater awakening.

Be Awakened

Approach me in your truth
and I'll predict your next move.
I see the future.

The world awakens.
Brothers and sisters
re-writing the rules
of reality.

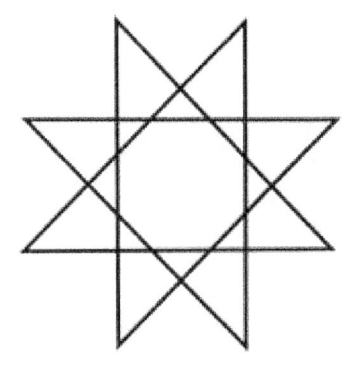

Chapter 8: Creation

Cosmic garden
Cosmic garden in the rainbow beam.
White light glows
blue and green;
Through soil, seeds and rain a
cosmic shine.
Radiating light that
births the mind.

Creators of Earth
They speak
ways of freedom,
wisdom of war.

Frightening stories
of love they fought for.

Which will one day, you'll see,
spread peace
through out the galaxy.

Violet Prison/ flame
The universe will be complete.
Is complete.
Has always been complete.
He dips the paintbrush in
compassion, love and unity.
Paints himself inside a violet prison.
Burns in a violet flame.

Thinking
Stillness in the field.
Life has come to yield.

Climbing cliffs, sit in thought.
Angels teach what they've been taught.

Observing earths disturbance.
Controlled, quite, deserted.

Is it just me?
The world feels
empty;

Unhappy.

Rhythm

My instrument controls the people.

And they dance
And they drink

Clap in rhythm, vibration is raised.

Smiling faces cheer as we sing loud
secrets of the universe to the crowd.

Music

All through pregnancy,
allow her beautiful
vibrations.

Mothers will sway their children
to sleep with rhythms of the universe.

Chemically Balanced

Make room for something more.
Remove
        fear
        anger
        pride
Build belief;
Start thinking clearly.

Developing
It wont be long.
New generations rise again and again.
Natures cycles cant be broken

New beliefs,
new knowledge.

In the eyes of children,
new colour.
Deeper meaning.
Further to understand what is.

Transformation
Entangle yourself in
what you wish to become.

Knowledge of music creates the musician.
It is transforming.

Manifesting
Found in light,
enchanting words
by seekers.

Pass through the ears of sleepers.
Writing out vibrations on paper.

> "Waken them from their sleep
> Wake me from this dream"

Mirroring the Creator
Create.
You will be created.

In the mirror,
the creator has recognized itself.

A dimension opens its eyes to see the new artist.

Up to Me
I have a thought and I have a vibration.

A thought of peace.
A vibration of happy and forwardness.

Stars step aside and allow me to guide life.

Elements move over in my favour.

Darkness leaves the third dimensional dome

and only light is found in this realm.

Search for the Right Words
For the perfect spell,
I've gone deep into the cosmos.

For the right words,
I've searched dreams.

Searching for the poetry
that sends us transcendent
and into peace.

Tool
Through greed, pain and desire,
even hell would come to order.

One would step up and rule.

Chaos into divinity
and those below
become the tool.

Moving Forward
I've come back
to set all free.

We can be anything
we want to be.

 If it rings in your heart
as true,
do anything you want to do.
But stop;
Think.
Is this moment now, reality?
Question it.
You'll see.

"Something, Something Invention"
There's a god man in the Southern woods,
some say.
He shouts into silence
twice a day.
 "Something, something, invention!"

Cosmic Alarm/ putting out the vibe
No noise would wake us now
in this idea of reality.
As one, we reach for the invention that awakens
the sleeping soul of earth.

                Life; Destined for awakening.

Foundation of Creation

Thought
Vibration
Matter
Thought
Vibration
Matter

Vibrations of Money
A small piece of the universe is in the shape of money.
In the shape of me.

"Money is bad.
The root of all evil"

Says the poor, angered men
who catch flies without honey.

Magical
What I reveal is
nothing more than a spell.
With your magical breath,
speak into the void
of yourself.

The Invention
Send me answers
Send me the invention
Send me the knowledge
I wish to learn
I have a plan
A way forward with man

Could You Imagine
A world where God is *all* religions.
Could you imagine
beings with no fear, or pride.
A species that collectively
discovered reason.
Imagine a space.
Imagine such a heaven.

Armed With a Paintbrush
Nothing gets by me!
No way!
No how!
Not now!

Standing taller with a paintbrush some how.

Painting Beings
As I dream,
I paint a new design.
I can feel un-imagined powers.
Unlimited and infinite.

Dip in midnight blue.
One thrust of the brush;
Vast emptiness
spread through.

Light years of canvas,
galaxies spilled like sand on the beach.
Off into the distance, Earth.
Trillions of ideas
in billions of beings.

Stars Within Reach
Put to paper, laws of the universe.
Mold them into a spell.
You can have anything you want;
Heaven or an unrealized hell.
My soul turns its cheek
at all things that hurt.

To have what you desire
see them as stars,
chemicals and atoms first.

Creating the Kingdom
With all your heart and passion,
breathe wishes into existence.
Enjoy the kingdom you create.

Truly Desire
What is it you truly desire?
Just say it.
Lets the process begin.
Let the magic in;
and be blown away
by how easy it is.

Desire to Write
My pen and paper hear and understand me.
Always listening.
No judgment,
no opinions;
Just listens.
It must come out.
Pent up energy waiting to come to life.

A Poem From The Galaxy
Pick it out of thin air.
It is already yours.
Let it be truthful.

It's getting the idea.

Hands reach out for the poem.

One from the universe.
Into the book that awakens all.

This is Heaven
Look around you.
To the left and to the right;
These are God's eyes.
A divine sight.
Is life exactly what you had hoped for?
Build your kingdom the way it must be built and more.

Heaven exists
in your vision.
Designed and painted
in your decision.

Take Your Seat/ perfect fit
It's your seat, after all.
Don't be afraid to take up the mantle.

It's your purpose.
Your invention.

Heart like a feather.
Land hands on fine leather.

Fancy new throne.

A perfect fit.

Where's My Paint Brush
Blind in dullness and darkness.
Light years of absence.

Nothing
Nothing
Nothing

Depression in my truest form.

Living Art
Every imaginable color hangs to dry
on the canvas recently painted.
Some smudges of imperfections
turned to stars and birds,
bushes, rain and mountains.
Colour of love;
Passion in pinks.
The artist paints himself in the corner
to live life
as the paint.
The brush,
canvas,
and hand.
A self creating universe.

Harmony
Suddenly, every bit of beauty
has come forward to show itself.
We stand as one.

One universe
One reality

Beauty;
Harmony.

In this one moment
we call existence.

Rest
I'll spend this time thinking.
To gather my thoughts.

So long I forgot my purpose.
My direction
Running and running
Never looked back, never stopping.

These feet, these arms
heart and mind,
worn and bruised
from the adventure.
Life is long.
My soul is tired.

Just for a minute,
I wish to close my eyes;
Bring the journey to and end.

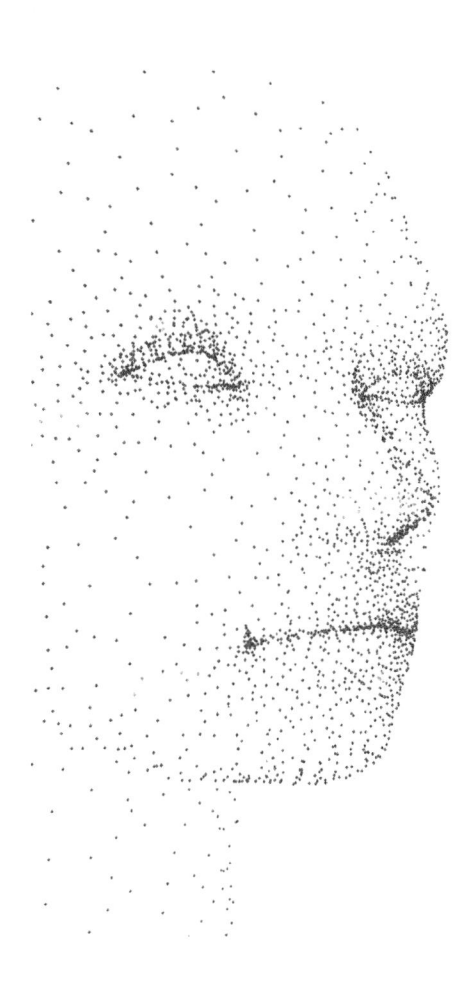

Chapter 9: Universe

Dreaming of Heaven
Dampened music in the mist
Stumbling upon an old molded village.
Forever, I have searched.

My neck follows inward on the sound
coming up from the steamy ground.

She takes my hand
down a foggy river.

Walked with me,
hypnotically.

Humidity hugs us;
Becomes us
in a floating sound cloud of our own.
Green, blue, luscious life
dances without wind.
Water, leaves, heat.
Lost in the dream that is heaven.

Fractal of Light
This is the universe.
And while we interpret meaning
behind fractals of light,
we lose ourselves in the illusions
that have always been truth.

Where's That Darn Brush Again
Brush. Brush.
Where did I put my brush?
Let me paint.
Rediscover the surprise to no end.
Where did I put that darn paint brush again?

Your Face in the Stars/ map
Galaxies light years away,
through the emptiness of space.
Like a light show,
stars draw in your beautiful face.

A map
illuminates the sky.
All with clues of purpose
as to why.

Breathing Universe/ reality
Inhale the stars.
Exhale in exchange.
In,
out,
the universe breathes.
In,
out,
my heart pulses with meaning.
I am reality.

Knowing
She prances like wind around seeds.
Delicately carry on the quest of need.

She sings into the elements
as a medium of stars,
freed.

And brings light to all beings.

They know who they are
in their divinity.

And wakes them
of insanity.

Entangled
Through music,
poetry and
dance;
Entangled with nature.
Deeper and deeper.
Not always through animals and trees
But stars and new realities.

Permanently Inspired
Your beauty has knocked me off my feet again.

Not once have I been surprised,
But blown away.

Like dancing with a paint brush.
You color reality in a new shade.

The One Who Awoke Me
In a moment of stillness,
brighter beam of light meet her eyes.

A Goddesses collection of all the stars;
Just for me.

Reaching out, saves me in darkness.
Insists I be free.

Deeply in Love
If you could live in my mind for a moment,
you would fall deeply in love.
Seduced by the beauty of all that is.
This moment
in creation.

Worthy
In all the universe, love stumbles upon me.
Am I worthy?
An inevitable unity.
Who else has received
these gifts of truth and belief?

Bound by nothing,

through sickness, stagnancy and hate
lives a stronger desire
to illuminate.

Balanced
Spinning like a ballerina on stage.
Knows conflict is man made.
Elegant;
Not at all afraid.
She keeps her balance
and is proud of the progress she made.

Stars Hold Her Up
Counting on love,
she walks with stars under her feet.
Never looking down.
Planets are her ground.
No chance in defeat.

Unconscious Enchantment
She doesn't realize enchantment
of performance.
Through touch, her fingertips send
energy into my skin.
The air she breathes turns reality into magic.
Enchants the bathtub with splashes and laughter.

A laughter quite contagious.
She is healing.

Dance, sing, encouragement;
works like a spell
for happiness and good health.

Smiling,
loving and playing
takes away sickness.
High vibrations of love and honesty.

Foolishly in Love/ change
Never again has wickedness
touched earth.
Angels strike ground
promising purity;
Change in our divinity.

Going Cosmic
Follow me to the place.
Enter the universe, mindfully,
Step forward, into infinity.

Honest Witch
Potions.
Believer of magic.
Searching for mushroom,
searching for mind.

Spells on broadcast
for love and peace.
Forever enchanting.

Fire Dancer
She absorbs the crowd;
Sways like leaves
and heat lights up her face.

Belly burns from experience.
Fearless to fire.
They are one thing.

Passion
Truth
Desire

No music needs playing.
Her hips are the sound.

Her circle chants her into trick.

Reflected flame in the eyes of awe
was a burning universe.

Flow
Perfection.
Disturbance stays hidden.
Did she find it forbidden?
Does the universe, herself, object?

She pulls me closer
with charm and dazzling stars.

Fell deep into her bright eyes.
Spit through the other side.
Ripped out my soul
and died.

This it is.
This is it, I'm dead.
Another round of eternity
coming at me like a train.

Wholeness,
in glowing beauty,
reaches out to my hand.

With a jerk,
pulls me into existence.
Softly, falling face to face.

She makes angels in wild flowers and sand.
Splashing leaves through out the garden.

Crashing ocean waves and
we sing while music flows into our veins.
Admiring the infinite beauty
in and around our being.

Nature's Rhythm
Time stops and colours glow vibrant.
Electric streaming flow of reality
swaying with natures rhythm.

Dances with thought.
Stops in her sudden realization.
"It's me."
Her eyes widen to the surprise.

Sparkle
The igniting spark
in lively eyes
A flame like suns that make up the universe.
Wider and brighter
than all else.

Stories of love
and loss in
expression;
Adventure.

Still, continues the journey
with a smile in search to find
whatever is found.

With no plans nearing end,
deeper discoveries of herself and then
pushing further.

Experiences all along the way.

Beat Down
Weight on my shoulders;
Weak from the world
searching for meaning.
Taken a toll, but knows
the truth
of the beating.
Mentally,
physically.

Forever
I'll catch you forever.

She walked the stars,
into my arms and we began
our eternal journey.

Divinely, dust will blow
upward
like a rising tornado
of soul into being.

I'll wait again, an eternity.

Body Language
Your feet face the door;
Anxiety.

Nervous;
The way you linger,
wanting more.

It shows;
Your energy is external.

And beautiful.

Lean in to tell me secrets.
I trust.
I glow.

Happiness radiates onto me.
Play, dance,
weep in my arms.

I see love
taking shape
of poetry.

Listening
What will you say to her?
Shes gentle;
Accepting.

Passion
Blow it into the universe and she will listen.
"I want to understand these truths.
I'm passionate of you"

Moving The Universe
Universe,
Now it's my turn to move *you*.
Imagination is all that I am.
Vowing to find truth in it all again.
Every intention to stay on track, but
Reality has thrown me for a loop and back.
She loses her balance
Ever so slightly.

Abyss
Staring deep into the abyss.
Sees the self as this.
Found in the mindful
void of emptiness.

Clearing heads of illusions.
Doubting splattered stars.
Deciding in freedom
to bend the bars.

All Light; Beauty
Truth of love
is the harmony of laughter.

Happiness.
Acceptance.

Beauty radiates all around you.
In every step
and breath you take.

Light that never goes away.

Breath of the Universe
As my body transforms into ground,
plants and memory; I live on.
In an old joke;
Laughter,
and in the breathe of everyone.

Woman of the Universe

A girl wants what she can't have.
So I give you the whole sky
and all the light you can grab.

Freckles like the uncountable stars on your face.
Screaming black holes, our eyes gravitate.
Investigate.
Cant pull away.
Every word I write sends her transcendent.

"I'm free"

Joyful tears roll off into my heart.

Bound by nothing and our souls kiss in a red room.

Love
Love;
Not what I was told.
Nothing here on earth I
would use to
describe.

Nothing short of God.

I love all that is, was and will be.
I love you, infinitely.

Ripple
Through now and all of earth;
The big picture of her existence.
Trickling from her heart, and into mine,
rippled a new vision throughout
all space and time.

Singing/ guidance
Ripples in the elements
are the voices of angels.

The higher being spill out troubles.

Through divine sound,
we hear her scars.
Language in perfect vibration.
Songs of learned lessons.

Lesson/ forgive me
I'm sorry for my ignorance.
In return,
we are freed in honor of
sadness and pain.
Forever, I'll look back and cry
now that I know what was in your eye.

Dying hurt.

Lesson learned.

Incomplete/ rightfully yours
Incomplete.
You have my heart
and I never stop thinking of you.
I want nothing.
How can I be whole, if you have my love?
Keep it forever.
My heart is rightfully yours.

Without Love
I am nothing.
I am everything.

Numb
Chasing love.
Desire;
I've been burned
Fell to ash.
but enjoy the pain every time.
I keep coming back.

Love again
Love taken from me
once more.
Do I cry over betrayal
Over and over?
Carry on a skeptic that love
is real?
Ripped from my arms
time and time again.
But perhaps love
can only be given.

Divine Order
Disguised as chaos, it may seem.
Perfection is a bumpy stream.
Intelligence unfolds
a life controlled,
and love's the only dream you hold.

Freed
Freed.
But see,
There's nothing for you
I wouldn't do,
If you'd
come back to me.

Push and pull/ letting go
Driven in and out of my arms,
I'm learning to let go.
An energy trade, we give and take.
Balance is the dance of us both.

Manipulation/ witch
Hip-fully
dancing through the doorway.
Snakes follow her in.
Light bulbs go out over her head
and eyes shined a piercing red.
What an energy.
What an entrance.

Show Yourself
I'm not the only one who knows.
Where are you
out in the star ocean?

Do you stand with me here
in a veiling fear?

A watching seer
in tears.
Guiding me all these years?

Breakthrough
Right in front of you;
This is a world for you, by you.
Building blocks for your kingdom.

Your playground.
No longer limited.

See's herself as one.
In a pit of nothingness
Ready to create
Easily moving reality.

Coming to Life
Celestial geometry
comes to life in dreams.
Planets danced around the being.

Taking shape of the new earth.

Builds an army of love.

Artists, poets and
truth seekers.

A war
evil can't win.

The wielding weapon;
Enchanting poetry.

Angel war cries on the field.
Wailed so, so beautifully.

Lets Be Human
Just for a day, show me what built you.
All of your flaws.
who you are.
Your old name and fears,
what brought you tears,
and be created by our conscious scars.

Alive
The universe
breathes on forever.
and in a fractal of dream and breath of being,
we are.

As one
Into the abyss,
drifting in a river of stars.
Deep,
deep
 nowhere.
My body tingles with static.

Floating there, in the air above care.
with a blissful, glowing stare.
Light and love everywhere.

Calling
No resistance to
the calling of my heart.

I hear your poem.
I hear you;
Reflecting in the stars.

I dream of a fantastic death, over and over with
you.
Our rebirth, search and rest.
In hopes
we meet again and again

Cosmic Creation

She lays on a bed of stars.
Her seductive stare draws me in.
Hourglass shape
and she shines.
She glows like a centered seed.
Compassion births new meaning,
new desires,
and a new cosmic vibration.

Smiling Back

Into the heart of earth,
smiles,
ear to ear
on all the happy beings.
Moving them with
laughter
and deeper meaning.

Greatest Invention/experience

Existence.
Life, search, rebirth
My greatest invention.

The whole universe fits in the palm of my hands.
Packed like sand
into something more than truth,
but a desire to experiences them all.

Journey/ wake up
All those hurting;
all those asleep,
flawed;
Part of the being
that is mind.

Imagination.

Perfection.

A timeless journey;

Now wake up
and enjoy the dream.

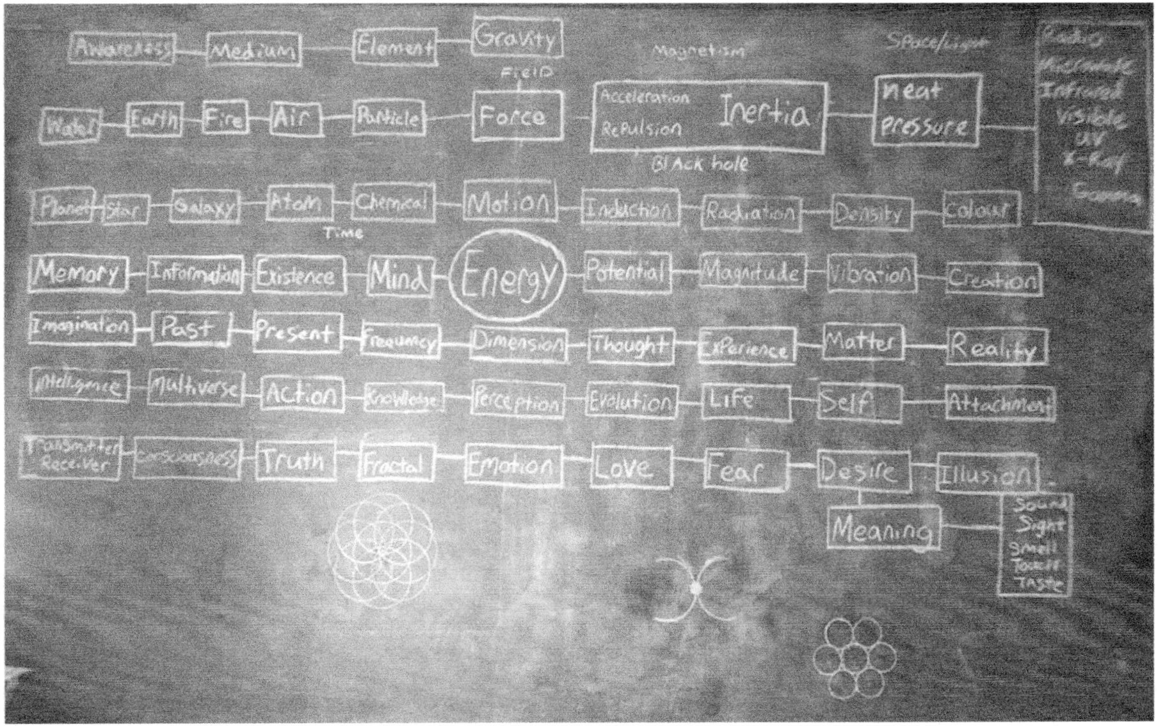

Awareness
Medium
Element
Gravity
Field
Magnetism
Space/Light
Water
Earth
Fire
Air
Particle
Force
Acceleration
Repulsion
Inertia
Heat
Pressure
Black hole
Radio
Microwave
Infrared
Visible
UV
X-Ray
Gamma
Planet
Star
Galaxy
Atom
Chemical
Motion
Induction
Radiation
Density
Colour
Time
Memory
Information
Existence
Mind
Energy
Potential
Magnitude
Vibration
Creation
Imagination
Past
Present
Frequency
Dimension
Thought
Experience
Matter
Reality
Intelligence
Multiverse
Action
Knowledge
Perception
Evolution
Life
Self
Attachment
Transmitter
Receiver
Consciousness
Truth
Fractal
Emotion
Love
Fear
Desire
Illusion
Meaning
Sound
Sight
Smell
Touch
Taste

Printed in Great Britain
by Amazon